Mr. Food® TEST KITCHEN

Quick & Easy

COMFORT

c o o k b o o k

Best-Selling Author with Millions of Cookbooks Sold

More Than 150 Mouthwatering Recipes

Recipes © 2011 by Cogin, Inc.
Main recipe photos © 2011 by Hal Silverman Studio, Inc.
Other photos © 2011 by Cogin, Inc.

Inquiries should be addressed to:
Cogin, Inc.
1770 NW 64 Street, Suite 500
Fort Lauderdale, FL 33309

Mr. Food, OOH IT'S SO GOOD!!, the trademarks, logos, and the Mr. Food likeness are registered marks owned by Ginsburg Enterprises Incorporated. All rights reserved.

Library of Congress Cataloging-in-Publication Data
Mr. Food
Mr. Food Quick & Easy Comfort Cookbook / Mr. Food

ISBN 978-0-9755396-2-0

1. Cookery. 2. Quick and Easy. I. Title: Mr. Food Quick & Easy Comfort Cookbook. II. Title.
Printed in the United States of America
First Edition
www.MrFood.com

introduction

Did you ever get a whiff of something baking in the kitchen and suddenly have a déjà vu moment? It probably triggered a fond food memory of a happy time. And can you recall an especially hectic day where you've been comforted by knowing you had a hearty meal to come home to? Comfort food recipes are the tried-and-true favorites that get passed down from generation to generation 'cause they make us feel good.

That's exactly why, for months, the Mr. Food Test Kitchen team tirelessly brainstormed, prepared and taste-tested lots of the all-time favorite nostalgic recipes folks like you are looking for. The result? Here in the pages of our Quick & Easy Comfort cookbook are more than 150 soul-soothing, back-to-basics recipes that'll surely make your day any day. Along with loads of mouthwatering photos, you'll find wholesome, satisfying meal ideas for breakfast, lunch, dinner, snacks, and entertaining, too. Like a favorite worn pair of jeans or a warm, cozy evening by the fire, these recipes will hug you from the inside out.

You don't need a ticket or a time machine to take your taste buds on a trip down memory lane! Just like a best friend, you can keep this copy of our Quick & Easy Comfort cookbook close at hand to help you make down-home favorites that have earned their place in mealtime history.

Old-fashioned comfort food never goes out of style 'cause, with the kitchen being the heart of most homes, these welcoming dishes will warm your heart as they make time stand still! And, from the aromas to the tastes, we know these will have you and yours saying... "OOH IT'S SO GOOD!!®"

Jodi   Howard   Art   Steve

Carol   Helayne   Patty   Caryl

Tina   Kelly   Ethel   Jaimé

Jeannie   Dave   Rosette

Pictured on front cover (l-r): Patty Rosenthal -Test Kitchen Director, Howard Rosenthal - Chief Food Officer, Art Ginsburg - aka Mr. Food, Kelly Rusin - Food Stylist/Photographer.

acknowledgments

We all have something in our lives that naturally means "comfort." To most of us, it's being surrounded by family or friends or a special "something" that conjures up warm memories. Sometimes it's a certain food that makes us feel extra-good and that, of course, has been the inspiration for this book.

Well, OUR greatest comfort, as the Mr. Food Team, is knowing we are surrounded by so many talented and caring people who have made putting this book together such a pleasure.

It's a true comfort knowing that we have had Patty Rosenthal to head up our Test Kitchen for the last 17 years. For countless cookbooks and thousands of TV segments, Patty has been the person who has made sure every recipe turns out "just so," while adhering to our quick & easy, tasty philosophy. We also want to tip our chef's hat to Jeannie Suits and Jaime Gross, who diligently tested and retested every recipe to make sure each one would bring you true comfort, and to Rosette Pierre and Dave DiCarlo for keeping our kitchen in tip-top shape.

Two key people on our editorial team whom we couldn't live without are Jodi Flayman and Helayne Rosenblum, who certainly helped make this book come together by adding lots of TLC to every page... you both are incredible! It's also comforting to know we have the talents of Carol Ginsburg and Caryl Ginsburg Fantel to proofread each and every word so it's just right for you.

When you find yourself drooling over all these full-page photos, the credit will have to go to Hal Silverman Studios. Hal and his production assistant, Frank Schram, are truly amazing, and a pleasure to work with! We also want to thank Kelly Rusin for capturing all the insert photos that brighten up our recipe pages. And for bringing everything to life, a big thank-you to Lorraine Dan, who took all the recipes and photos and magically transformed them into a truly memory-making cookbook. What a team!

For making sure everything always runs smoothly, we salute Steve Ginsburg, CEO, who heads up the administrative side of our business, along with Lina Nin, our Controller. And, of course, where would we be without Ethel Ginsburg, aka "Mrs. Food"? Ethel keeps Mr. Food looking his very best and always in the right place at the right time.

True comfort comes from knowing that Howard Rosenthal, our COO, is there every step of the way to help steer the team with his creative vision, and for challenging all of us to make everything we do truly spectacular.

Last, but certainly not least, our biggest comfort of all is knowing we are inspired everyday by the founder of the Mr. Food Brand, Art Ginsburg. Art not only drew the map that we all follow, but his quick & easy philosophy has been instilled in each of us. Thank you for sharing all your gifts with us.

We also want to thank all the other people who, in one way or other, helped create such a warm and tasty cookbook. You know who you are...and you know how much we appreciate all you do.

But the most important thanks go to you, our viewers and readers, who have shared so much of yourselves with our team over the years, and who make everything we do so rewarding. The greatest comfort of all is your loyalty, and for that we are truly grateful.

contents

notes

cozy breakfasts

crispy french toast

serves 4

---

4 cups coarsely crushed cornflakes cereal

1/4 cup sugar

1 teaspoon ground cinnamon

7 eggs

1/4 cup milk

1 teaspoon vanilla extract

1 (1-pound) loaf egg bread (challah), cut into 8 (1-inch) slices

1/3 cup vegetable oil

1 In a shallow dish, combine crushed cereal, sugar, and cinnamon; mix well and set aside.

2 In another shallow dish, beat eggs, milk, and vanilla.

3 Dip one slice of bread in egg mixture, coating both sides, then place in cereal mixture, coating both sides. Repeat with remaining bread.

4 In a large skillet, heat oil over medium heat. Cook bread slices 2 to 4 minutes on each side, or until golden. Remove to a paper towel-lined platter and cover to keep warm.

Note:

Serve immediately with syrup or your favorite fresh fruit.

Just a Thought:

What happens when you combine your favorite cold cereal with your favorite skillet breakfast? You'll find out after just one bite...and we think you'll be pleasantly surprised!

buttermilk waffles

makes 6 waffles

2 cups all-purpose flour

3 tablespoons sugar

1 teaspoon baking powder

1 teaspoon baking soda

1/2 teaspoon salt

2 eggs, beaten

2 cups buttermilk (see Tip)

4 tablespoons butter, melted

1 Preheat an electric waffle iron according to directions. Coat with cooking spray.

2 In a large bowl, combine flour, sugar, baking powder, baking soda, and salt. Stir in eggs, buttermilk, and melted butter; mix well (see Note).

3 Using a 1/2-cup measure, pour batter onto bottom of prepared waffle iron. Close lid and cook 60 to 90 seconds, or until golden.

4 Using a fork, carefully remove waffle to a plate. Repeat with remaining batter. Serve immediately.

Note:

For a change of pace, try adding 1 teaspoon almond extract to the batter to give it a little extra punch of flavor.

Don't have buttermilk on hand? Don't worry! Just add 2 tablespoons of either white vinegar or cream of tartar to 2 cups milk. Stir and let sit for about 5 minutes then use in place of the buttermilk in this or any other recipe. Is that easy or what?

chocolate chip pancake stack

serves 4

2 cups biscuit baking mix

1 cup club soda

2 eggs

1 teaspoon sugar

1 cup (6 ounces) semisweet chocolate chips

2 tablespoons vegetable shortening, divided

1 In a large bowl, combine biscuit baking mix, club soda, eggs, and sugar; mix well. Stir in chocolate chips until well combined.

2 On a nonstick griddle or in a large skillet, melt 1 tablespoon shortening over medium heat.

3 Pour 1/4 cup batter per pancake onto griddle and cook about 2 minutes, or until bubbles appear on top of each pancake. Flip pancakes and cook 1 to 2 minutes more, or until golden on both sides, adding more shortening to skillet as needed.

4 Serve immediately, or keep warm in a low oven until all pancakes are cooked.

Serving Suggestion:

Top each stack of pancakes with a dollop of whipped cream and sprinkle on some additional chocolate chips... Yummy!

Did You Know?

The secret ingredient in these light and fluffy pancakes is the club soda. You see, its carbonation incorporates air into the batter, making the pancakes lighter...just the way we remember them.

dutch apple pancakes

serves 4

3 eggs

1/2 cup all-purpose flour

1/2 cup milk

2 tablespoons (1/4 stick) butter, melted

1/2 teaspoon salt

1 tablespoon butter

1/2 cup packed light brown sugar

1/4 teaspoon ground cinnamon

1 (20-ounce) can sliced apples in water, drained

Confectioners' sugar for dusting

1 Preheat oven to 400°F. Coat 2 (9-inch) cake pans with cooking spray.

2 In a medium bowl, mix eggs, flour, and milk with an electric mixer; beat until smooth. Add the 2 tablespoons melted butter and the salt; beat well then pour mixture into prepared cake pans, distributing evenly.

3 Bake 10 minutes then reduce heat to 350°F. and bake 5 to 7 more minutes, or until puffy and golden.

4 Meanwhile, in a medium skillet, melt remaining 1 tablespoon butter over medium heat. Stir in remaining ingredients, except confectioners' sugar, and heat 3 to 5 minutes, until apples are heated through.

5 Remove pancakes to a serving platter then spoon half the apple mixture over each pancake, dust generously with confectioners' sugar, and serve immediately.

Just a Thought:
These Dutch classics are not your ordinary pancakes. They're comfort food at its best. Wait 'til you see how they make you feel!

ham & cheddar pinwheels

makes 16 rolls

1 cup diced cooked ham

1 cup (4 ounces) Cheddar cheese

4 scallions, thinly sliced

2 (8-ounce) packages refrigerated
crescent rolls (8 rolls each)

1 Preheat oven to 400°F. Coat a baking sheet with cooking spray.

2 In a medium bowl, combine ham, cheese and scallions; mix well.

3 Unroll one package of crescent rolls and press seams together to form one large rectangle. Repeat with second package of crescent rolls.

4 Sprinkle half the mixture evenly over each rectangle. Starting from a narrow end, roll up jelly-roll style. With a sharp knife, cut each roll into 8 equal slices and place each slice, cut-side down, on prepared baking sheet.

5 Bake 20 to 25 minutes, or until crust is golden. Serve warm.

Serving Suggestion:

These are great as a dinner roll, snack, salad go-along, or even just for breakfast.

Just a Thought:

This may not be how you remember having ham and cheese when you were growing up, but comfort food comes in all shapes and sizes. These pinwheels are so amazing, we think they just might become part of a new breakfast tradition in your house.

veggie frittata

serves 4 to 5

8 eggs, beaten

1 cup chopped fresh or
 frozen broccoli, thawed

1 small onion, chopped

1 small red bell pepper, chopped

1/4 cup (1 ounce) grated
 Cheddar cheese

1/4 teaspoon salt

1/4 teaspoon black pepper

1/4 teaspoon dried oregano

1/4 teaspoon dried basil

2 tablespoons butter

1 In a large bowl, combine all ingredients except butter; mix well.

2 In a 10-inch nonstick skillet, melt butter over medium heat. Pour egg mixture into hot skillet. Reduce heat to medium-low, cover, and cook until egg mixture is set, about 25 minutes.

3 Loosen frittata from skillet with a spatula and carefully slide onto a platter. Cut into wedges and serve immediately.

amish breakfast casserole

serves 12

2 (7-ounce) boxes fully cooked
 sausage links, cut into
 1/2-inch chunks

1 onion, chopped

6 eggs, lightly beaten

1 (2-pound) bag frozen shredded
 hash brown potatoes, thawed

2 cups (8 ounces) shredded
 Cheddar cheese

1-1/2 cups small curd cottage cheese

1-1/4 cups shredded Swiss cheese

1 Preheat oven to 350°F. Coat a 9" x 13" baking dish with cooking spray.

2 In a large skillet, cook sausage and onion over medium-high heat for 4 to 5 minutes, or until onion is tender.

3 In a large bowl, combine remaining ingredients; stir in sausage mixture. Transfer to prepared baking dish.

4 Bake, uncovered, for 35 to 40 minutes, or until set and golden. Let stand 10 minutes before cutting.

Did You Know?

The Amish generally eat only foods produced in their gardens or from their own farms. Many of their recipes also tie into long-standing family traditions. That's why we think this tried-and-true version of our Amish Breakfast Casserole will take you back to a simpler time.

peekaboo eggs

serves 4

4 slices Italian bread

2 tablespoons butter, softened

4 eggs

Salt to taste

Black pepper to taste

1 Preheat a griddle or large skillet over medium heat.

2 Cut a 2-1/2-inch hole in the center of each slice of bread, using a round cookie cutter or a paring knife. Evenly spread butter on both sides of the bread then place on griddle.

3 Crack an egg into the hole in each slice of bread. Sprinkle with salt and pepper.

4 Cook 1 to 2 minutes, or until bread is golden. Using a spatula, flip each slice and cook until desired doneness.

Just a Thought:

On days when you're feeling under the weather, our Peekaboo Eggs might be just what you need to bring a smile to your face.

crispy candied bacon

makes 12 slices

1 cup packed light brown sugar

12 slices thick-cut or regular sliced bacon

1 Preheat oven to 325°F. Line a baking sheet with aluminum foil.

2 Place brown sugar in a shallow dish. Press bacon into sugar, coating both sides evenly. Place on baking sheet.

3 Bake 20 to 25 minutes, or until bacon is crisp and brown sugar is caramelized. Let cool 2 minutes then serve.

farm stand hash browns

serves 4 to 6

1/4 cup olive oil

1 (2-pound) bag frozen cubed hash brown potatoes

1 red bell pepper, chopped

1 onion, chopped

2 cups sliced fresh mushrooms

1 teaspoon salt

1/2 teaspoon black pepper

2 cups fresh spinach

1 In a large skillet, heat oil over high heat.

2 Add potatoes, and cook 10 to 12 minutes, or until lightly browned.

3 Add bell pepper, onion, mushrooms, salt, and black pepper. Cook 6 to 8 minutes, or until veggies are tender, stirring occasionally. Add spinach and cook 1 minute; serve immediately.

Just a Thought:

America was built on farming, and our farm stands today are an extension of that, which is why we love paying them a visit to bring home fresh produce for recipes like our hearty Farm Stand Hash Browns.

soul-soothing grits

serves 5 to 6

3-1/2 cups water

1 cup white or yellow grits

1 cup shredded sharp Cheddar cheese

4 tablespoons butter

1/4 cup milk

1/4 cup real bacon bits

1/2 teaspoon salt

1/4 teaspoon black pepper

1/8 teaspoon ground red pepper

1 In a large saucepan, bring water to a boil over high heat. Add grits, and cook 5 to 7 minutes, or until mixture is thick, stirring occasionally.

2 Remove from heat and add cheese and butter; stir until cheese is melted.

3 Add remaining ingredients, and stir until well combined. Serve immediately, or place in a muffin tin coated with cooking spray, and chill. Just before serving, heat in a preheated 350°F. oven 15 to 20 minutes.

Did You Know?

To a Southerner, grits are a mainstay, and breakfast without grits is unthinkable. So, if you want the true taste of the South, make sure that you give our grits a try.

cinnamon raisin bread

serves 6

- 12 frozen dinner roll dough pieces, thawed and cut into 1-inch pieces
- 1 egg, beaten
- 3/4 cup packed light brown sugar
- 2 teaspoons ground cinnamon
- 1/2 cup raisins

1 Coat a 9" x 5" loaf pan with cooking spray; set aside. In a large bowl, toss dough pieces with egg. Stir in brown sugar and cinnamon; mix well. Place dough pieces on cutting board and cut into smaller pieces. Place back in bowl and stir in raisins until combined.

2 Spoon mixture into prepared pan and cover with plastic wrap. Let rise to top of pan, about 1-1/2 hours.

3 Preheat oven to 350°F. Remove plastic from pan, and bake 25 to 30 minutes, or until bread is golden. Let cool 5 to 10 minutes then remove from pan, slice, and serve warm as is or toasted with butter.

If you grew up eating homemade cinnamon raisin toast, do not pass on this recipe. It's the best, especially after it's slightly cooled, thickly sliced, buttered and toasted in a skillet or on a griddle.

pecan sticky buns

makes 9 buns

1/2 cup packed light brown sugar, divided

3 tablespoons butter, melted, divided

1 tablespoon light corn syrup

3/4 cup chopped pecans, divided

1 (8-ounce) package refrigerated crescent rolls

1 teaspoon ground cinnamon

1 Preheat oven to 375°F. Coat an 8-inch square baking dish with cooking spray.

2 In a small bowl, combine 1/4 cup brown sugar, 2 tablespoons melted butter, and the corn syrup; mix well until smooth then spread over bottom of prepared baking dish. Sprinkle with 1/2 cup pecans.

3 Unroll crescent dough and press seams together to form one large rectangle. Brush with remaining melted butter. Sprinkle with remaining brown sugar, the cinnamon, and remaining pecans.

4 Starting at a wide end, roll up dough jelly-roll style. With a sharp knife, cut into 9 equal slices and place each cut-side down in baking dish.

5 Bake 18 to 20 minutes, or until puffed and golden. Remove from oven and immediately invert onto a serving platter. Be careful...the melted sugar is very hot. Allow to cool slightly then serve warm.

Just a Thought:

We have no scientific research to back this up, however, our taste-testers insist that this recipe is addictive and can cause long-term happiness, uncontrollable smiles and even relieve some forms of stress.

coffee cake muffins

makes 12 muffins

1/2 cup (1 stick) butter, softened

1-1/4 cups sugar, divided

2 eggs

2 cups all-purpose flour

1 teaspoon baking powder

1 teaspoon baking soda

1/8 teaspoon salt

1 cup sour cream

2 teaspoons vanilla extract

1/2 cup chopped pecans

3/4 teaspoon ground cinnamon

1 Preheat oven to 350°F. Coat a 12-cup muffin tin with cooking spray.

2 In a large bowl, cream butter and 1 cup sugar with an electric beater on medium speed. Add eggs and beat until fluffy. Mix in flour, baking powder, baking soda, and salt. Add sour cream and vanilla; mix well. Fill each cup of muffin tin with 1 heaping teaspoon of batter.

3 In a small bowl, combine pecans, cinnamon, and remaining sugar. Sprinkle 1/2 teaspoon pecan mixture over batter then spoon another heaping teaspoon of batter over pecan mixture. Top with 1/2 teaspoon pecan mixture.

4 Bake 18 to 20 minutes, or until a wooden toothpick inserted in center comes out clean. Remove muffins from pan and cool on wire rack.

Just a Thought:

Not only are these muffins better than your average coffee cake but, since they're portable, they're the perfect companion to your on-the-go morning coffee. You can't get any better than that!

soups & chilis

tomato 'n' grilled cheese soup

serves 6

2 (28-ounce) cans crushed tomatoes

1 tablespoon sugar

1/2 teaspoon garlic powder

1 teaspoon salt

1 teaspoon black pepper

2 cups (1 pint) heavy cream

2 slices homestyle white bread

1 tablespoon butter, softened

1/4 cup shredded Cheddar cheese

1 In a large soup pot, combine tomatoes, sugar, garlic powder, salt, and pepper; bring to a boil over medium-high heat, stirring occasionally. Reduce heat to low and slowly stir in heavy cream. Simmer 5 to 7 minutes, or until heated through. Do not allow to boil.

2 Toast bread, evenly spread with butter, then cut into 1-inch pieces. Place 3 pieces on each serving of soup then sprinkle with cheese. Serve immediately.

Just a Thought:

Grilled cheese sandwiches and tomato soup make a classic comfort combo, so we decided to roll the tastes of both into one dish. What do you think?

loaded potato soup

serves 4 to 6

2 tablespoons butter

1 celery stalk, finely diced

1 small onion, finely diced

3 cups chicken broth

4 large potatoes, peeled and diced

3 tablespoons all-purpose flour

2-1/2 cups milk

1/4 teaspoon salt

1 teaspoon black pepper

2 cups (8 ounces) shredded
Cheddar cheese

1/2 cup bacon bits

1/2 cup finely sliced scallions

1 In a soup pot, melt butter over medium-high heat. Add celery and onion; sauté 5 to 7 minutes, or until tender.

2 Add chicken broth and potatoes; cover and bring to a boil. Reduce heat to low and simmer 20 to 25 minutes, or until potatoes are tender.

3 Add flour, milk, salt, and pepper; cook until soup is thickened and heated through, stirring constantly. Add cheese, bacon bits, and scallions; stir until cheese is melted. Serve immediately.

chunky manhattan clam chowder

serves 6 to 8

4 slices bacon, minced

2 celery stalks, chopped

2 medium carrots, chopped

1 large onion, chopped

3 medium potatoes, peeled and diced

2 (14-1/2-ounce) cans crushed tomatoes, undrained

2 (10-ounce) cans baby clams, undrained

2 (8-ounce) bottles clam juice

1 teaspoon dried thyme

1 In a soup pot, cook bacon 3 to 5 minutes over high heat, until crisp. Add celery, carrots, and onion; sauté 5 to 7 minutes, or until onion is tender, stirring frequently.

2 Add remaining ingredients, cover, and bring to a boil. Reduce heat to low and simmer, covered, 55 to 65 minutes, or until potatoes are very tender.

Readers Share Memories:

"I grew up in the Bronx and remember going to a luncheonette in the city to get the best clam chowder. Those were the days!" — Joe M., Syosset, NY

super creamy mushroom soup

serves 4 to 6

4 tablespoons (1/2 stick) butter

1 pound fresh mushrooms, sliced

1 small onion, chopped

1/2 teaspoon salt

1/8 teaspoon black pepper

5 tablespoons all-purpose flour

4 cups chicken broth

1 cup half-and-half

1/4 teaspoon browning and
   seasoning sauce

1 In a soup pot, melt butter over medium heat. Add mushrooms, onion, salt, and pepper; sauté until tender.

2 Add flour and cook 2 to 3 minutes, stirring constantly. Gradually add broth and bring to a boil then reduce heat to low and simmer 10 minutes, stirring occasionally.

3 Slowly stir in half-and-half and browning sauce and simmer 5 more minutes, or until thickened. Serve immediately.

Note:
If you have leftovers and want to reheat this, warm it over low heat, stirring occasionally.

Lighter Comfort:
Replace the half-and-half with 1% milk and use low-sodium chicken broth. That'll save you about 75 calories, 8g fat, and 280mg sodium per serving.

aunt mary's veggie soup

serves 10

6 cups beef broth

1 (20-ounce) can cannellini beans, undrained

1 (28-ounce) can crushed tomatoes, undrained

1 (10-ounce) package frozen chopped spinach, thawed

1 (16-ounce) package frozen mixed vegetables

1 small onion, chopped

1 teaspoon garlic powder

1 teaspoon salt

1/2 teaspoon black pepper

1 cup uncooked ditalini pasta (or other small shape)

1 In a large soup pot, combine all ingredients except pasta. Bring to a boil over medium-high heat then stir in pasta.

2 Reduce heat to low and simmer 15 minutes, or until pasta is tender, stirring occasionally.

Just a Thought:

Even if you don't have an Aunt Mary, we think you'll find our Aunt Mary's Veggie Soup "souper" soothing. Maybe serve it the way she did by topping each bowl with a little grated Parmesan cheese. It'll give every spoonful an extra-rich taste.

chicken & dumplings

serves 6

3 celery stalks, sliced

2 carrots, sliced

8 cups chicken broth

1/2 teaspoon poultry seasoning

1/4 teaspoon black pepper

2 cups biscuit baking mix

2/3 cup milk

3 cups chopped or pulled cooked chicken

1 Coat a soup pot with cooking spray and heat over medium-high heat. Add celery and carrots; sauté 6 minutes, or until tender. Stir in broth, poultry seasoning, and pepper; bring to a boil.

2 Meanwhile, in a medium bowl, stir together biscuit baking mix and milk until blended. Turn dough out onto a heavily floured surface; roll or pat dough to 1/8-inch thickness. Cut into 1" x 3" strips.

3 Drop strips, one at a time, into boiling broth mixture; stir in chicken. Cover, reduce heat to low, and simmer 8 to 10 minutes, stirring occasionally, until dumplings are cooked through.

Lighter Comfort:

You can reduce the sodium in this Southern classic without sacrificing taste. Substitute low-sodium chicken broth for its regular counterpart to lower the sodium by more than 370mg per serving.

homemade chicken soup

serves 6 to 8

1 (2-1/2- to 3-pound) chicken,
cut into 8 pieces

10 cups cold water

4 carrots, cut into 1-inch chunks

3 celery stalks, cut into
1-inch chunks

2 onions, cut into 1-inch chunks

3 tablespoons chicken base
(see Tips)

1 tablespoon salt

1-1/2 teaspoons black pepper

1 In a soup pot, combine all ingredients and bring to a boil over high heat. Reduce heat to low; simmer 1-1/2 hours, or until the chicken easily falls off the bones.

2 Using tongs, remove chicken from soup; allow chicken to cool slightly. Bone and skin the chicken, cut meat into 1-inch chunks, and return it to the soup.

Note:

For homemade matzo ball soup, prepare matzo balls (opposite page) and add them to the soup pot about 15 minutes before serving.

Not familiar with chicken base? It can be found next to the bouillon in the supermarket. Also, we suggest making this in advance so you have time to refrigerate it overnight. The fat from the chicken can then be skimmed off the top of the soup before reheating and serving.

aunt sarah's matzo balls

makes about 1 dozen

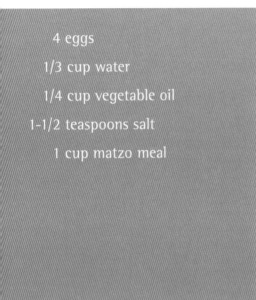

4 eggs

1/3 cup water

1/4 cup vegetable oil

1-1/2 teaspoons salt

1 cup matzo meal

1. In a large bowl, combine eggs, water, oil, and salt; mix well. Add matzo meal, and stir just until combined; do not overmix.

2. Cover and chill 30 minutes. Remove matzo ball mixture from refrigerator; wet your hands slightly, and form mixture into 1-inch balls.

3. Meanwhile, bring a large pot of water to a rolling boil over medium-high heat. Carefully drop matzo balls into boiling water; cover and cook 20 minutes, or until balls float to the top and are completely cooked inside.

4. Remove matzo balls with a slotted spoon and place in a shallow baking dish. Cover and chill until ready to reheat in a pot of chicken soup. Or, to serve immediately, remove matzo balls from their cooking pot and add to a pot of hot chicken soup about 15 minutes before serving.

Just a Thought:

If you've ever had matzo balls, you know that sometimes they're firm, and other times they're light and fluffy. Aunt Sarah's are right in between.

grandma's split pea soup

serves 6 to 8

4 cups water

4 cups beef broth

1 pound fully cooked boneless ham, cut into 1/2-inch chunks (see Tips)

1 (24-ounce) package dry green split peas

2 onions, chopped

2 carrots, cut into chunks

2 celery stalks, cut into chunks

1 teaspoon salt

1 teaspoon black pepper

1 In a large soup pot, combine all ingredients over medium-high heat; bring to a boil.

2 Reduce heat to low, cover, and simmer 50 to 60 minutes, or until vegetables are tender.

You can use leftover ham or buy it right from the deli case. And if the soup becomes too thick after it has been chilled, as it often does, just stir in a little water when rewarming it to achieve the desired consistency.

deli-style beef barley soup

serves 8

8 cups beef broth

6 carrots, diced

4 onions, chopped

1 pound mushrooms,
   thinly sliced

1 pound stew beef, cut into
   1/2-inch chunks

1/2 teaspoon salt

1/2 teaspoon black pepper

1 cup quick-cooking barley

1 In a soup pot, combine broth, carrots,
onions, mushrooms, stew beef, salt, and pepper.
Bring to a boil over medium-high heat,
stirring occasionally.

2 Reduce heat to low; simmer, partially covered,
for 40 to 50 minutes, or until beef is tender,
stirring occasionally.

3 Add barley, and cook, partially covered,
for 15 to 20 minutes, or until barley is tender.

3-bean turkey chili

serves 6

1 pound ground turkey breast

1 onion, chopped

1 green bell pepper, chopped

1 teaspoon chopped garlic

1 (16-ounce) can black-eyed peas, rinsed and drained

1 (16-ounce) can navy beans, rinsed and drained

1 (15-ounce) can red kidney beans, rinsed and drained

3 (14-1/2-ounce) cans diced tomatoes, undrained

2 tablespoons chili powder

1 teaspoon ground cumin

1 teaspoon salt

1 teaspoon black pepper

1 Coat a soup pot with cooking spray. Add turkey, onion, bell pepper, and garlic. Cook over medium-high heat 5 to 7 minutes, until no pink remains in turkey, stirring occasionally to break it up.

2 Add remaining ingredients. Bring to a boil, stirring occasionally. Reduce heat to low, cover, and simmer 20 minutes.

Just a Thought:

Easy preparation is one ingredient that has to be included in all our "comfort" recipes. Since this chili uses everyday, off-the-shelf pantry staples, it's satisfying on all levels.

saucy white chili

serves 8

1 tablespoon vegetable oil

6 skinless, boneless chicken breast halves (1-1/2 to 2 pounds total), cut into 1-inch cubes

1/4 teaspoon salt

1/4 teaspoon black pepper

1 onion, chopped

1 teaspoon minced garlic

5 (16-ounce) cans Great Northern beans, undrained

1 (14-1/2-ounce) can whole tomatoes, undrained, broken up

1 (4-ounce) can chopped green chilies, undrained

3-1/2 cups chicken broth

2 teaspoons ground cumin

1 teaspoon chili powder

1 In a soup pot, heat oil over medium heat. Sprinkle chicken with salt and pepper; sauté 5 to 6 minutes, until browned. Add onion and garlic, and cook 3 to 4 minutes, or until onion is tender. Add remaining ingredients; bring to a boil.

2 Reduce heat to low and simmer 50 to 60 minutes, or until chili thickens slightly, stirring occasionally.

Serving Tip:
For a really hearty meal, I like to serve this chili in a big bowl over hot cooked rice.

Did You Know?
Not all chilis are created equal! Maybe that's why there are more than 400 chili cook-offs held throughout the U.S. every year. As a matter of fact, almost every region of the country has its very own version of chili. This version has everything a winning recipe needs, except all the usual calories and fat.

very veggie chili

serves 6 to 8

1 tablespoon olive oil

1 large onion, chopped

1 (28-ounce) can crushed
   tomatoes, undrained

2/3 cup picante sauce

1-1/2 teaspoons chili powder

1-1/2 teaspoons ground cumin

3/4 teaspoon salt

2 (15-ounce) cans red kidney
   beans, rinsed and drained
   (see Note)

1 large red bell pepper,
   chopped

1 large zucchini,
   cut into 1/2-inch chunks

1 medium-sized yellow squash,
   cut into 1/2-inch chunks

1 In a large saucepan, heat oil over medium heat.
   Sauté onion 2 to 3 minutes.

2 Add tomatoes, picante sauce, chili powder, cumin,
   and salt. Reduce heat to low, cover, and simmer
   10 minutes. Add remaining ingredients, cover,
   and simmer 10 more minutes.

Note:
*For a change of pace, I often like to use black beans
instead of red kidney beans, so go ahead, mix 'em,
match 'em...use your favorite.*

Just a Thought:
*If you're trying to get finicky eaters to eat their veggies, try this chili. You'll be thrilled when they
eat every last drop.*

touchdown chili

serves 8

2 pounds ground beef

1/2 onion, chopped

2 (15-ounce) cans red kidney beans, undrained

2-1/2 cups tomato sauce

1 (8-ounce) jar salsa

4 tablespoons chili seasoning mix

1 teaspoon granulated garlic

1/2 teaspoon salt

1 teaspoon black pepper

1. In a soup pot, combine ground beef and onion over medium heat; sauté 10 minutes, or until meat is browned and onion is tender. Drain excess liquid.

2. Add remaining ingredients to soup pot; mix well. Reduce heat to low and simmer 45 to 50 minutes, until chili begins to thicken.

For all you slow cooker fans...after browning the ground beef, as directed above, add beef and remaining ingredients to a 4-4.5 quart slow cooker. Cook on low for 6 to 8 hours, or on high for 4 hours, and dinner is done whenever you need it.

Readers Share Memories:

"Every time I eat chili, I remember when my mom used to make a batch and the whole family would enjoy it with yummy corn bread. Good times, and good memories!"
— *Alice R., Colorado Springs, CO*

texas-style chili

serves 4

1/4 cup vegetable oil

3 pounds lean beef chuck roast, well trimmed and cut into 1-inch cubes

1 onion, chopped

3 garlic cloves, minced

3 tablespoons chili powder

2 teaspoons ground cumin

2 teaspoons salt

2 teaspoons hot pepper sauce

3 cups water

1 (4-ounce) can chopped green chilies, drained

1 In a large saucepan, heat oil over medium-high heat; add beef, and cook 5 minutes. Drain off excess liquid. Add onion and garlic, and sauté 5 minutes, until beef is browned on all sides and onion is tender, stirring frequently.

2 Stir in chili powder, cumin, salt, and hot pepper sauce; cook 1 minute. Add water and chilies, and bring to a boil, stirring occasionally. Reduce heat to low, cover, and simmer 45 minutes, then remove cover and simmer 45 more minutes, or until beef is fork-tender.

Note:

This is great served over hot cooked rice, garnished with chopped onions, shredded cheese, and sour cream. Mmm mmm!

Did You Know?

True Texas-style chili is made with chunks of beef, not ground beef, and it never contains beans. In Texas, this is true comfort!

notes

casseroles & stews

grandma's macaroni and cheese

serves 6

1 (16-ounce) package elbow macaroni

2 (10.75-ounce) cans condensed Cheddar cheese soup

2 cups milk

6 cups (1-1/2 pounds) shredded sharp Cheddar cheese, reserving 1 cup for topping

3 tablespoons butter, melted

1-1/2 teaspoons dry mustard

1 teaspoon salt

3/4 teaspoon black pepper

1 Preheat oven to 350°F. Coat a 9" x 13" baking dish with cooking spray.

2 Cook macaroni according to package directions; drain and place back into pot. Stir in remaining ingredients except reserved cheese.

3 Pour mixture into prepared baking dish and sprinkle with reserved cheese. Bake 35 to 40 minutes, or until heated through.

Readers Share Memories:

"Mac and cheese at Grandma's house is one of my earliest food memories. It's warm and tender, just like Grandma's love for me!"
—*Carol L., Elgin, PA*

unstuffed pork chops

serves 6

6 boneless pork chops

6 (1-ounce) slices Swiss cheese

1/4 pound fresh mushrooms, sliced

1 (10-3/4-ounce) can condensed cream of celery soup

1/2 cup dry white wine

2 cups pork-flavored stuffing mix

4 tablespoons (1/2 stick) butter, melted

1 Preheat oven to 350°F. Coat a 9" x 13" baking dish with cooking spray.

2 Place pork chops in prepared baking dish. Top each pork chop with a slice of Swiss cheese. Arrange sliced mushrooms over cheese.

3 In a small bowl, mix together soup and wine; pour over pork. Sprinkle stuffing mix over the top, and drizzle on melted butter.

4 Bake 35 to 40 minutes, or until pork is no longer pink in center.

Did You Know?
Any boneless cutlet can be interchanged in most recipes. For example, once in a while, chicken or turkey cutlets would be a nice change of pace in this one, instead of the pork chops.

tempting turkey tetrazzini

serves 6

8 ounces uncooked spaghetti

1-3/4 cups chicken broth

8 ounces fresh mushrooms, sliced (about 3 cups)

2 cups low-fat milk

3 tablespoons cornstarch

1/4 cup dry white wine or water

1/2 teaspoon salt

1/2 teaspoon black pepper

3 cups coarsely chopped cooked turkey breast (about 1 pound) (see Tip)

1/4 cup Italian-style bread crumbs

1 Cook spaghetti according to package directions; drain and set aside.

2 In a soup pot, bring broth to a boil over medium-high heat. Stir in mushrooms then reduce heat to medium-low and simmer 4 to 5 minutes, or until mushrooms are tender. Stir in milk.

3 In a small cup, combine cornstarch and wine, and stir until smooth; slowly pour into mushroom mixture. Increase heat to medium and bring to a boil, stirring constantly.

4 Remove pot from heat and stir in salt, pepper, and turkey. Add spaghetti and toss until well coated.

5 Preheat oven to 375°F. Coat a 9" x 13" baking dish with cooking spray. Spoon spaghetti mixture into prepared baking dish and sprinkle evenly with bread crumbs. Bake 20 to 25 minutes, or until golden and bubbly.

Don't think that you have to roast a whole turkey to make this. No, sir. Do what our test kitchen does...buy a 1-pound chunk in the deli and cut it up yourself. Our recipes are all about making good food that's quick and easy.

satisfying shepherd's pie

serves 6 to 8

1 pound lean ground beef

1 onion, chopped

1 (1.15-ounce) envelope onion soup mix

1 (12-ounce) jar beef gravy

1 teaspoon garlic powder

1/2 teaspoon black pepper

1 cup frozen whole-kernel corn, thawed

1-1/2 cups frozen sliced carrots, thawed

1 cup frozen peas, thawed

5 cups prepared mashed potatoes

Paprika for sprinkling

1 Preheat oven to 350°F. Coat a 2-quart casserole dish with cooking spray.

2 In a large skillet, brown ground beef and onion. Drain excess liquid, if necessary. Add soup mix, gravy, garlic powder, and black pepper; mix well. Add corn, carrots, and peas.

3 Place mixture in prepared casserole dish. Spread mashed potatoes over the top and sprinkle with paprika.

4 Bake 30 to 35 minutes, or until heated through.

Did You Know?

In England, this wouldn't be considered Shepherd's Pie. The British call it Cottage Pie, since authentic Shepherd's Pie is actually made with chunks of lamb. It'll be fun to share this bit of trivia when serving up this casserole.

one-pot chicken gumbo
serves 6 to 8

1 pound bacon, chopped

1-1/2 pounds boneless, skinless chicken breasts, cut into 1-inch chunks

1-1/2 pounds boneless, skinless chicken thighs, cut into 1-inch chunks

1 (28-ounce) can diced tomatoes, undrained

1 (16-ounce) package frozen whole-kernel corn, thawed

1 (16-ounce) package frozen cut okra, thawed

3-1/2 cups chicken broth

1 teaspoon salt

1 teaspoon black pepper

1/2 teaspoon hot pepper sauce

1 In a soup pot, cook bacon over medium heat 10 to 12 minutes, or until crisp, stirring occasionally; drain off fat.

2 Add remaining ingredients and bring to a boil. Reduce heat and simmer 35 to 40 minutes, or until chicken is no longer pink and gumbo has thickened, stirring occasionally.

Just a Thought:
When you think of comfort in New England, you might think of chowder. In the South, it's Chicken and Biscuits. On the Bayou...you guessed it, "comfort food" has everybody thinking of gumbo.

seaside seafood stew

serves 4 to 6

2 tablespoons olive oil

6 scallions, thinly sliced

1/4 cup chopped fresh parsley

4 garlic cloves, chopped

1 (15-ounce) can crushed tomatoes, undrained

1 (15-ounce) can diced tomatoes, undrained

1 cup dry white wine

2 teaspoons sugar

1/2 teaspoon salt

1/2 teaspoon black pepper

1 pound white-fleshed fish (like haddock, cod or tilapia), cut into 1-inch chunks

1/2 pound uncooked shrimp, peeled and deveined, tails left on

1 In a soup pot, heat olive oil over medium-high heat. Add scallions, parsley, and garlic; cook 2 minutes. Stir in crushed and diced tomatoes, the wine, sugar, salt, and pepper. Reduce heat to low and simmer 10 minutes.

2 Stir in fish and shrimp, cover, and cook 6 to 8 minutes, or until fish flakes easily with a fork.

frogmore stew

serves 4 to 6

8 cups water

2 tablespoons seafood seasoning

1/2 teaspoon salt

1/4 teaspoon ground red pepper

1 pound kielbasa sausage, cut into 2-inch pieces

6 potatoes, cut in half

6 onions, peeled and cut in half

3 ears of corn, cut into 3-inch pieces

1 pound large shrimp, unpeeled

1 In a soup pot, combine water, seafood seasoning, salt, and pepper. Bring to a boil over high heat then add sausage, potatoes, onions, and corn. Cook 15 to 20 minutes, or until potatoes are fork-tender.

2 Add shrimp and cook 2 to 3 minutes, or until shrimp are pink and cooked through. Strain the stew and serve immediately, along with bowls of broth for dunking.

Did You Know?

Relax, there are NO frogs in Frogmore Stew. In fact, Frogmore Stew is more of an event than a dish 'cause it's usually served by spreading newspaper over a picnic table and dumping it all out. Everybody just helps themselves. It's South Carolina comfort food at its best.

wintry baked beef stew

serves 6

2 pounds beef stew meat,
cut into 1-inch chunks

4 large carrots, cut into
1-inch chunks

4 potatoes, peeled and cut
into 1-inch chunks

1 onion, chopped

2 cups tomato juice

1 cup water

3 tablespoons quick-cooking
tapioca

1 teaspoon sugar

1 teaspoon salt

1/2 teaspoon black pepper

1 Preheat oven to 350°F. Coat a 9" x 13" baking dish or 2-quart roaster with cooking spray.

2 In a large bowl, combine beef, carrots, potatoes, and onion. In a medium bowl, combine tomato juice, water, tapioca, sugar, salt, and pepper; mix well. Pour tomato mixture over beef mixture; mix well then pour into prepared baking dish and cover with aluminum foil.

3 Bake 2 to 2-1/4 hours, or until beef is tender.

Just a Thought:

We shared this tummy-warming recipe on TV and would be remiss if we didn't include it in this collection, since we got such an outpouring of positive feedback. You won't find a better, easier beef stew recipe anywhere.

curried lamb stew

serves 6 to 8

1/2 cup (1 stick) butter

2-1/2 to 3 pounds boneless leg
of lamb or lamb stew meat,
cut into 1-inch chunks

2 onions, chopped

3 tablespoons all-purpose flour

1 cup beef broth

2 apples, cored, peeled, and
coarsely chopped (see Tip)

1 cup raisins

1 tablespoon curry powder

1 teaspoon salt

1/4 teaspoon black pepper

1 In a large skillet, melt butter over medium-high heat. Sauté lamb chunks and onions 12 to 15 minutes, or until no pink remains in the lamb. Stir in flour then broth. Add remaining ingredients; mix well.

2 Reduce heat to low, cover, and simmer 1 hour, or until meat is fork-tender.

Granny Smith apples are one of the best types to use for this because they're a little firmer and hold up well to heat. They're ideal for many of our memory-making recipes like apple pie and cobblers, to name just a few.

good ol' american goulash

serves 4 to 6

1-1/2 to 2 pounds ground beef

1/2 green bell pepper, chopped

1 small onion, chopped

1 (28-ounce) jar spaghetti sauce

1 teaspoon garlic powder

1 teaspoon salt

1/2 teaspoon black pepper

8 ounces uncooked elbow macaroni

1/2 cup water

1 cup (4 ounces) shredded mozzarella cheese

1 Preheat oven to 350°F. Coat a 2-1/2-quart casserole dish with cooking spray.

2 In a large skillet, brown ground beef, bell pepper, and onion over medium-high heat 6 to 8 minutes, or until no pink remains in the beef, stirring frequently. Drain off excess liquid. Add remaining ingredients except cheese; mix well.

3 Place in prepared casserole dish, cover, and bake 25 minutes. Remove from oven and top with mozzarella cheese. Return to oven and bake, uncovered, 15 to 20 minutes, or until heated through and cheese has melted.

Just a Thought:

This is a perfect dish to make ahead and freeze for anytime you need a quick meal. You can even freeze it in individual portions so the kids can microwave a dish after school.

italian tortellini stew

serves 8

1 tablespoon vegetable oil

1 carrot, finely chopped

1 celery stalk, finely chopped

1 onion, chopped

1 (28-ounce) can crushed tomatoes, undrained

1 (15.5-ounce) can Great Northern beans, drained and rinsed

4 cups chicken broth (see Tips)

2 tablespoons dried basil

1/4 teaspoon salt

1/4 teaspoon black pepper

2 zucchini, cut into 1/2-inch chunks

1 (8-ounce) package dried cheese-filled tortellini (see Tips)

1 In a soup pot, heat oil over medium heat. Add carrot, celery, and onion; cook 5 minutes, stirring occasionally.

2 Stir in tomatoes, beans, chicken broth, basil, salt, and pepper. Bring to a boil then reduce heat to low, cover, and simmer 30 minutes.

3 Add zucchini and tortellini then return to a boil; reduce heat to low and simmer, uncovered, for 15 minutes, or until tortellini are tender.

If you're looking to make this vegetarian, simply substitute vegetable broth for the chicken broth. Also, refrigerated or frozen tortellini can be used, however, you'll need to adjust the cooking time accordingly.

four-cheese pasta

serves 4 to 6

2 tablespoons vegetable oil

1 small onion, finely chopped

2 (14-1/2-ounce) cans diced tomatoes, drained

1 teaspoon dried basil

1/2 teaspoon salt

1/2 teaspoon black pepper

1/2 pound ziti or bow tie pasta

1 cup ricotta cheese

4 slices (4 ounces) mozzarella cheese

4 slices (4 ounces) Swiss cheese

6 slices (6 ounces) provolone cheese

1 Preheat oven to 350°F. Coat a 9" x 13" baking dish with cooking spray.

2 In a large saucepan, heat oil over medium-high heat. Add onion, reduce heat to low, and cook, stirring occasionally, just until tender but not browned. Stir in tomatoes, basil, salt, and pepper, and cook 10 minutes. Remove from heat and set aside to cool slightly.

3 Meanwhile, cook pasta according to package directions; drain.

4 Spoon a thin layer of the tomato mixture in the prepared baking dish then layer 1/3 of the pasta, all the ricotta cheese, the mozzarella cheese, another 1/3 of the pasta, all the Swiss cheese, then the remaining pasta and remaining tomato mixture. Top with provolone cheese.

5 Cover and bake 30 minutes, or until mixture is hot and bubbly. Let sit 10 minutes before serving.

How about trying whole-grain pasta in this recipe? With all the cheesy goodness, they'll never even notice, plus it will add about 3g of fiber per serving!

spinach and cheese manicotti

serves 4

8 ounces uncooked manicotti shells

Cooking spray

1 (32-ounce) container part-skim ricotta cheese

2 cups (8 ounces) shredded mozzarella cheese

1/2 cup grated Parmesan cheese, divided

1 egg, beaten

1/4 teaspoon salt

1/4 teaspoon black pepper

1 (10-ounce) package frozen chopped spinach, thawed and squeezed dry

1 (16-ounce) jar spaghetti sauce

1 Preheat oven to 350°F. Coat a 9" x 13" baking dish with cooking spray.

2 Prepare manicotti shells according to package directions; drain, rinse, and drain again. Spray pasta lightly with cooking spray.

3 In a large bowl, combine ricotta cheese, mozzarella cheese, 1/4 cup Parmesan cheese, the egg, salt, and pepper. Add spinach; mix well.

4 Fill each manicotti shell with about 1/3 cup of the cheese mixture (see below) then place them in prepared baking dish. Pour spaghetti sauce over shells and sprinkle with remaining Parmesan cheese. Bake 35 to 40 minutes, or until hot throughout.

Did You Know?

We spray the manicotti shells with cooking spray to prevent them from sticking. Also, there's an easy way to fill manicotti shells. Many restaurants even do it this way: Place the cheese mixture in a resealable plastic storage bag, snip off a corner of the bag, and gently squeeze the cheese mixture into each shell.

layered ravioli bake

serves 8

2 (26-ounce) jars spaghetti sauce

1 (9-ounce) box frozen chopped spinach, thawed, squeezed dry

2 (22-ounce) bags frozen square cheese ravioli (see Tips)

3 tablespoons grated Parmesan cheese

3 cups (12 ounces) shredded mozzarella cheese

1 Preheat oven to 375°F. Coat a 9" x 13" baking dish with cooking spray.

2 Spread 1 cup spaghetti sauce on bottom of prepared baking dish. Sprinkle 1/3 of spinach over sauce, layer 1/3 of ravioli on next, then sprinkle with 1 tablespoon Parmesan cheese. Pour 1 cup spaghetti sauce on top then evenly distribute 1 cup mozzarella cheese over sauce.

3 Repeat layers 2 more times, ending with sauce, reserving the last cup of mozzarella cheese until after baking.

4 Cover with aluminum foil and bake 50 to 60 minutes, or until hot in center.

5 Remove cover and sprinkle with remaining 1 cup mozzarella cheese. Heat 5 more minutes, or until cheese is melted. Let sit 5 minutes before slicing and serving.

For an even heartier meal, you can use beef ravioli instead. And, to keep foil from sticking to the top of any casserole, spray it with cooking spray before placing it over the food. That's how we do it, and it works every time.

award-winning lasagna

serves 6 to 8

12 lasagna noodles

1 pound ground beef

4 cups (16 ounces) shredded mozzarella cheese, divided

1 (15-ounce) container ricotta cheese

1/3 cup plus 2 tablespoons grated Parmesan cheese, divided

1 egg

1/2 teaspoon Italian seasoning

1/2 teaspoon black pepper

2 (28-ounce) jars spaghetti sauce

1 Preheat oven to 375°F. Coat a 9" x 13" baking dish with cooking spray. Cook and drain lasagna noodles according to package directions.

2 Meanwhile, in a large skillet, cook ground beef over medium-high heat until no pink remains, stirring to break up beef as it cooks. Drain off excess liquid and set aside.

3 In a large bowl, combine 3 cups mozzarella cheese, the ricotta cheese, 1/3 cup Parmesan cheese, the egg, Italian seasoning, and pepper; mix well.

4 Spread 1 cup spaghetti sauce evenly over bottom of prepared baking dish. Place 3 noodles over sauce. Sprinkle one-third of the meat then 1/3 of the cheese mixture over noodles. Pour 1 cup spaghetti sauce over cheese mixture. Place 3 more noodles over the top and press down lightly.

5 Repeat with 2 more layers of the meat, cheese mixture, sauce, and noodles. Spoon remaining sauce over the top and cover tightly with aluminum foil. Bake 1 hour.

6 Remove foil and sprinkle remaining mozzarella cheese and Parmesan cheese over top; return to oven for 5 more minutes, or until cheese is melted. Remove from oven and allow to sit 10 to 15 minutes before slicing and serving.

country-style chicken potpie

serves 6

---

2 tablespoons butter

1 pound boneless, skinless chicken breast halves, cut into 1/2-inch chunks

3/4 teaspoon salt

1/2 teaspoon black pepper

1 (16-ounce) package frozen peas and carrots

1 (14-1/2-ounce) can whole potatoes, drained and cut into 1/2-inch chunks

1 (12-ounce) jar chicken gravy

1 (15-ounce) package rolled refrigerated pie crusts

1 In a large skillet, melt butter over medium-high heat. Sprinkle chicken with salt and pepper, and sauté 4 to 6 minutes, or until no pink remains. Remove from heat and add peas and carrots, potatoes, and gravy; mix well.

2 Preheat oven to 400°F. Unroll 1 pie crust and place it in a 9-inch deep-dish pie plate, pressing crust firmly into plate. Spoon chicken mixture into crust.

3 Unfold second pie crust and place it over chicken mixture. Pinch edges together to seal; flute and trim as needed. Using a sharp knife, cut four 1-inch slits in top crust.

4 Bake 40 to 45 minutes, or until filling is heated through and crust is golden. Allow to sit 10 minutes before serving.

Since this potpie gets really hot and bubbly, we suggest placing a cookie sheet under it while baking, to catch any drippings. This recipe shouldn't be the reason you clean your oven!

four-layer chicken divan

serves 6

1/2 teaspoon salt

1/2 teaspoon black pepper

6 boneless, skinless chicken breast halves

1 (14-ounce) package frozen broccoli florets, thawed

2 (10-3/4-ounce) cans cream of chicken soup, undiluted

1/2 cup mayonnaise

3/4 cup (3 ounces) shredded sharp Cheddar cheese

1 cup coarsely crushed butter-flavored crackers

2 tablespoons butter, melted

1 Preheat oven to 350°F. Coat a 9" x 13" baking dish with cooking spray.

2 Sprinkle salt and pepper evenly over chicken and place in prepared baking dish. Distribute broccoli evenly over chicken.

3 In a medium bowl, combine soup, mayonnaise, and cheese; mix well then pour over broccoli. In a small bowl, combine crackers and butter then sprinkle over soup mixture.

4 Bake, uncovered, 40 to 45 minutes, or until no pink remains in chicken.

Lighter Comfort:

Want to enjoy this dish but trying to eat a bit lighter? We suggest using reduced-fat soup and cheese, light mayonnaise, and buttery spread to save about 135 calories, 17 grams fat, and 99 mg sodium per serving.

simple tuna noodle casserole

serves 4

1 (16-ounce) package medium egg noodles

2 (10-3/4-ounce) cans condensed cream of mushroom soup

2-1/2 cups milk

2 (12-ounce) cans tuna, drained and flaked

1-1/2 cups frozen peas

3 tablespoons melted butter, divided

1 teaspoon salt

1/2 teaspoon black pepper

1-1/2 cups kettle-cooked potato chips, crushed

1 Prepare noodles according to package directions; drain.

2 Preheat oven to 350°F. Coat a 9" x 13" baking dish with cooking spray.

3 In a large bowl, combine soup and milk; mix well. Add noodles, tuna, peas, 2 tablespoons melted butter, the salt and pepper; mix well.

4 Pour into prepared baking dish and top evenly with potato chips. Pour remaining melted butter over chips.

5 Bake 35 to 40 minutes, or until heated through. Serve immediately.

Note:
If you want to make this in advance, just put it together and keep it chilled until ready to top with the crushed potato chips and bake; adjust cooking time accordingly.

Just a Thought:
What a great way to use up those leftover broken potato chips in the bottom of the bag! They work well in lots of recipes for things like breading chicken or topping casseroles, like we do here. Yup, crushed potato chips deliver just the right crunch and flavor we need for loads of our favorite dishes.

ham and potato casserole

serves 6

---

2 (10-3/4-ounce) cans condensed cream of celery soup

3 cups milk

1/2 teaspoon onion powder

1/2 teaspoon salt

1/2 teaspoon black pepper

1 pound fully cooked boneless ham, cut into 1/2-inch chunks

1 (30-ounce) package frozen shredded hash brown potatoes, thawed

1 (10-ounce) package frozen peas

1 Preheat oven to 375°F. Coat a 9" x 13" baking dish with cooking spray.

2 In a large bowl, combine soup, milk, onion powder, salt, and pepper; mix well. Stir in remaining ingredients, pour into prepared baking dish, and cover tightly with aluminum foil.

3 Bake 30 minutes then uncover and bake 55 to 60 more minutes, or until hot and bubbly.

Just a Thought:
This soothing dish goes together in a flash and will surely make your family feel loved. Convenience foods never tasted so good!

hot dog 'n' bean casserole

serves 6

1 pound hot dogs, sliced into
1/4-inch diagonal slices

2 (14-ounce) cans vegetarian
baked beans, drained

2 tablespoons light brown sugar

1 tablespoon ketchup

1 cup (4 ounces) shredded
Monterey Jack cheese

1 Preheat oven to 375°F. Coat an 8-inch square baking dish with cooking spray.

2 In a large bowl, combine all ingredients except the cheese; mix well. Pour into prepared baking dish.

3 Cover baking dish tightly with aluminum foil and bake 20 to 25 minutes, or until heated through. Remove foil, sprinkle with cheese, and cook 10 more minutes, or until cheese is melted.

Did You Know?

All our recipes are tested, tasted and re-tested to make sure they're easy to make and yummy to our taste buds. Talk about kid-friendly...this recipe pleased even the most finicky eaters in our test kitchen.

pepperoni lasagna pizza

serves 6 to 8

12 lasagna noodles

4 cups (16 ounces) shredded mozzarella cheese, divided

1 (3-ounce) package sliced pepperoni

1/4 pound fresh mushrooms, sliced

2 cups spaghetti sauce

1-1/2 teaspoons Italian seasoning

1 Preheat oven to 375°F. Coat a 10" x 15" baking sheet with cooking spray.

2 Cook noodles according to package directions then drain; pat dry with paper towels. Place 6 noodles crosswise on prepared baking sheet, cutting noodles to fit, if necessary. Sprinkle 2 cups cheese over noodles. Layer pepperoni and mushrooms over cheese.

3 Cover with 6 more noodles placed in same crosswise direction. Spread sauce over noodles, cover with remaining 2 cups cheese, and sprinkle with Italian seasoning.

4 Coat one side of a large piece of aluminum foil with cooking spray and cover baking sheet with coated side toward lasagna (so cheese won't stick); bake 20 to 25 minutes, or until pasta is heated through and cheese is melted.

Just a Thought:

Most of us have fond childhood memories of traditional lasagna and pizza. Now we can combine the two to get the ultimate meal!

hearty main dishes

mama's meat loaf

serves 6

1-1/2 pounds ground chuck

1/3 cup finely chopped onion

1/2 cup Italian bread crumbs

1 egg

2/3 cup ketchup, divided

1/2 teaspoon salt

1/2 teaspoon black pepper

1 Preheat oven to 350°F. Coat a rimmed baking sheet with cooking spray.

2 In a large bowl, combine all ingredients except 1/3 cup ketchup; mix well.

3 Place mixture on prepared baking sheet and form into an oval (football) shape. Spread remaining 1/3 cup ketchup evenly over top.

4 Bake 1 to 1-1/4 hours, or until juices run clear. Allow to sit 5 minutes then slice and serve.

Readers Share Memories:
"Meat loaf and mashed potatoes are the comfort foods in our house. They just warm the body and soul."
— Nancy R., Seneca, NY

meat loaf mexicana

serves 6

1-1/2 pounds ground chuck

1/3 cup salsa

1/2 cup plain bread crumbs

1 egg

2 tablespoons taco seasoning

1/4 cup (1 ounce) shredded
   Cheddar cheese

1 Preheat oven to 350°F. Coat a rimmed baking sheet with cooking spray.

2 In a large bowl, combine all ingredients except the cheese; mix well. Place mixture on prepared baking sheet and form into an oval (football) shape.

3 Bake about 1 hour, or until juices run clear. Remove from oven, sprinkle with cheese, then bake 5 more minutes, or until cheese is melted. Allow to sit 5 minutes then slice and serve.

Note:
How 'bout serving this with a homemade Pico de Gallo salsa that tastes fresh-picked from the garden? See recipe below.

Just a Thought:
Just 'cause it's a classic homey favorite doesn't mean meat loaf is boring. Our south-of-the-border spin on the basic recipe will be a fiesta for your taste buds!

pico de gallo

makes about 3 cups

2 ripe tomatoes, finely chopped

1/2 onion, finely chopped

3 fresh jalapeño peppers, stems and
   seeds removed, finely chopped

1 tablespoon chopped fresh cilantro

1/4 teaspoon salt

Juice of 1/2 lime

1 In a large bowl, combine all ingredients; mix well. Cover and chill at least 1 hour, or until ready to serve.

old world stuffed cabbage

serves 6 (makes 12 rolls)

1 large cabbage, cored

1 (28-ounce) can crushed tomatoes, undrained

3 tablespoons light brown sugar

1 tablespoon Worcestershire sauce

1 pound ground beef

1 cup cooked rice, cooled

1 small onion, chopped

1 egg

1 teaspoon salt

1/2 teaspoon black pepper

1 Preheat oven to 350°F. Coat a 9" x 13" baking dish with cooking spray.

2 In a large saucepan, bring 1 inch of water to a boil over high heat. Place cabbage in water, cored-side down; cover pan and reduce heat to low. Steam for 20 minutes, or until cabbage leaves pull apart easily. Drain and set aside.

3 In a medium bowl, combine tomatoes and their juice, brown sugar, and Worcestershire sauce; mix well and set aside. In a large bowl, combine ground beef, rice, onion, egg, salt, pepper, and 2 tablespoons of the tomato mixture; mix well.

4 Place 1 cup tomato mixture in bottom of prepared baking dish. Peel a cabbage leaf off the head and cut off the thick stem end. Place 1/4 cup meat mixture in center of leaf. Starting at core end, make a roll, folding over sides and rolling loosely. Place seam-side down in baking dish; repeat with remaining cabbage leaves and meat mixture. Spoon remaining tomato mixture evenly over tops of cabbage rolls.

5 Cover and bake 1-1/4 hours. Uncover and cook 10 more minutes, or until beef is no longer pink.

old-fashioned stuffed peppers

makes 6 stuffed pepper halves

1 (26-ounce) jar spaghetti sauce, divided

1 pound ground beef

1 cup uncooked instant rice

1-1/2 cups (6 ounces) shredded mozzarella cheese, divided

1/4 cup water

1 tablespoon grated Parmesan cheese

1 teaspoon garlic powder

1/2 teaspoon salt

1/4 teaspoon black pepper

3 large bell peppers, washed, tops removed, sliced in half, and seeded

1 Preheat oven to 400°F. Spread 1 cup spaghetti sauce on bottom of 9" x 13" baking dish.

2 In a large bowl, combine ground beef, rice, 1 cup mozzarella cheese, 1 cup spaghetti sauce, the water, Parmesan cheese, garlic powder, salt, and black pepper; mix well.

3 Stuff each bell pepper half with an equal amount of meat mixture and place in prepared baking dish. Pour remaining spaghetti sauce evenly over stuffed peppers.

4 Cover and cook 40 to 45 minutes, or until no pink remains in meat and rice is tender. Remove from oven, uncover, and sprinkle with remaining 1/2 cup mozzarella cheese.

5 Bake 5 more minutes, or until cheese is melted. Spoon sauce over peppers, and serve.

Just a Thought:

These all-in-one, high-fiber, little edible bowls are a tried-and-true memory-making easy main dish. Why not jazz up your table with the colors of the rainbow by mixing and matching the colors of your peppers?

beefed-up spanish rice

serves 4 to 6

2 tablespoons vegetable oil

1 pound ground beef

1 small onion, chopped

1 green bell pepper, chopped

2 cups cooked rice

1 (26-ounce) jar spaghetti sauce

1 teaspoon garlic powder

3/4 teaspoon salt

1/2 teaspoon black pepper

1 In a large skillet, heat oil over medium-high heat. Add beef, onion, and green pepper. Cook 7 to 9 minutes, or until meat is browned, stirring occasionally; drain liquid.

2 Stir in remaining ingredients, reduce heat to low, and simmer 10 to 15 minutes, or until heated through.

Serving Suggestion:

How 'bout making this in individual crocks, topping them with shredded mozzarella cheese, then baking them until the cheese is all melty? That way, each person gets their own dish.

potluck spaghetti & meatballs

serves 4 to 6

1-1/2 pounds ground chuck

1/2 cup Italian bread crumbs

1/4 cup grated Parmesan cheese

1 teaspoon garlic powder

1 egg

1/4 cup water

2 teaspoons Worcestershire sauce

1/2 teaspoon salt

1/2 teaspoon black pepper

2 (26-ounce) jars spaghetti sauce

1 pound spaghetti

1 In a large bowl, combine all ingredients except the sauce and spaghetti. Mix well then form into 15 meatballs.

2 Place meatballs in a large pot and cook over medium-high heat until brown on all sides, turning occasionally; drain.

3 Add spaghetti sauce, bring to a boil, then reduce heat to low and simmer 30 minutes, or until no pink remains.

4 Meanwhile, prepare spaghetti according to package directions. Serve cooked spaghetti with meatballs and sauce.

Just a Thought:

Have you ever been to an all-you-can-eat spaghetti supper at a church or firehouse? This potluck favorite conjures up tasty memories, so why not recreate them tonight at your own table?!

texas chicken-fried steak

serves 4

4 beef cubed steaks
   (1 to 1-1/4 pounds total),
   pounded to 1/4-inch
   thickness

1/4 cup Worcestershire sauce

1 cup all-purpose flour

1/2 teaspoon salt

1/2 teaspoon black pepper

3/4 cup buttermilk

1/2 cup vegetable oil

1-1/4 cups milk

1/4 cup chicken broth

1. In a large resealable plastic storage bag, marinate cubed steaks in Worcestershire sauce for 30 minutes in the refrigerator.

2. Place flour, salt, and pepper in a second bag and pour buttermilk into a third bag.

3. Place each steak in bag with flour, and shake to coat completely; coat each steak with buttermilk then with flour again.

4. In a large deep skillet, heat oil over medium-high heat until hot but not smoking. Add steaks and cook 3 to 4 minutes per side, until cooked through and coating is golden. Drain on a paper towel-lined platter and cover to keep warm.

5. Add 1/3 cup of the remaining seasoned flour to the skillet. Cook 2 to 3 minutes, or until flour is browned, stirring constantly. Whisk in milk and broth, stirring until thickened. Serve gravy over steak.

Whenever marinating or breading food, we recommend using resealable plastic gallon-sized bags so your hands won't get sticky, and cleanup is a cinch.

really tender pot roast

serves 6 to 8

1 tablespoon olive oil

1 (3-pound) boneless beef
  chuck roast

1 teaspoon salt

1/2 teaspoon black pepper

2 cups coarsely chopped onion

1 cup dry red wine

1/2 teaspoon dried thyme

2 teaspoons chopped garlic

2 cups beef broth

1 bay leaf

4 large carrots, cut diagonally
  into 1-inch pieces

2 pounds potatoes, peeled and
  cut into 2-inch pieces

1. Preheat oven to 350°F.

2. Heat olive oil in a Dutch oven, on the stovetop, over high heat (see note). Sprinkle roast with salt and pepper. Add roast and cook 5 minutes, turning to brown on all sides. Remove roast from pan. Add onion to pan; sauté 8 minutes, or until tender.

3. Return roast to pot. Add wine, thyme, garlic, broth, and bay leaf; bring to a simmer. Cover pot and bake in the oven for 1-1/2 hours, or until roast is almost tender.

4. Add carrots and potatoes to pot. Cover and bake 1 more hour, or until vegetables are tender. **REMOVE BAY LEAF FROM POT; DISCARD.** Slice roast across the grain (see Tip on page 82) and serve with vegetables and pan juices.

Did You Know?

The first metal cooking vessels that resemble today's Dutch ovens were used in the Netherlands in the 17th century, hence the name. Our modern versions are similar, simply thick-walled (usually cast iron) cooking pots with tight-fitting lids. They're often used for recipes that require long cooking either on the stovetop or in the oven, or both in the same recipe. Be sure that the pot you use is oven-proof.

asian-style pot roast

serves 6 to 8

1/3 cup vegetable oil

1/3 cup soy sauce

2 tablespoons honey

2 garlic cloves, chopped

1-1/4 teaspoons ground ginger

1 (2- to 3-pound) boneless beef chuck roast

4 medium carrots, sliced into 1-inch pieces

3 celery stalks, sliced into 1-inch pieces

2 onions, quartered

1/4 cup cold water

1 tablespoon cornstarch

1 Combine oil, soy sauce, honey, garlic, and ginger in a large resealable plastic storage bag; seal and shake to combine ingredients. Add beef, seal bag, and marinate in the refrigerator for 1 hour.

2 Place beef and marinade in a Dutch oven. Cover and bring to a boil over high heat. Reduce heat to low and simmer 1 hour. Add carrots, celery, and onions. Cover and simmer about 1-3/4 hours more, or until meat and vegetables are tender. Remove meat and vegetables to a platter; cover to keep warm.

3 Combine cold water and cornstarch; add to pan juices. Cook and stir until thickened. Slice the meat across the grain (see Tip on page 82). Serve gravy over meat and vegetables.

Note:

It's easy to switch this up and make a sweet-and-sour version by simply adding a drained, 16-ounce can of pineapple chunks with the carrots.

Just a Thought:

We're taking the mystery out of fusion cooking by injecting Asian flavors into our all-American pot roast for a hearty East meets West one-pot meal.

garlicky steak

serves 2 to 4

2 (12-ounce) T-bone steaks

1/4 teaspoon salt

1/4 teaspoon black pepper

1/4 cup (1/2 stick) butter

1 tablespoon chopped garlic

1 tablespoon chopped
fresh parsley

1 Season steaks on both sides with salt and pepper.

2 Using a large skillet or grill pan, brown steaks over medium-high heat 2 to 3 minutes per side, in batches if necessary.

3 Remove skillet from heat for 1 minute to cool slightly; reduce heat to low. Add butter, garlic, and parsley. Cook steaks 1 to 2 more minutes per side, or until desired doneness. Serve immediately.

Readers Share Memories:

"One of my best food memories is ordering a garlic steak at this fun little restaurant called the Bubble Room on Sanibel Island, Florida. You get a sizzling platter with the steak that's slathered in garlic butter. It's one of my favorites!"
— Kim L., Chicago, IL

double onion brisket

serves 6 to 8

1 (4- to 6-pound) beef brisket

2 (10-1/2-ounce) cans onion soup

2 large onions, thinly sliced

1 Preheat oven to 350°F. Coat a large roasting pan with cooking spray; place brisket in pan fat-side up.

2 Pour onion soup over brisket. Top with onions.

3 Cover tightly with aluminum foil and bake 3-1/2 to 4 hours, or until meat is fork-tender. Slice across the grain (see Tip) and serve topped with sauce from pan.

When carving, make sure you cut the brisket across the grain. When sliced with the grain, it will become stringy. When carved properly, "across" or against the grain, it will be very tender.

30-minute beef stroganoff

serves 4 to 6

2 tablespoons butter

1-1/2 pounds boneless beef top sirloin steak, thinly sliced across the grain

1 small onion, chopped

1/2 teaspoon salt

1/2 teaspoon black pepper

1/2 pound fresh mushrooms, cut into 1/2-inch slices

2 (12-ounce) jars beef gravy

1/2 cup sour cream

1 pound wide egg noodles, cooked according to package directions

1 In a large skillet, melt butter over medium-high heat. Add steak, onion, salt, and pepper, and cook 5 to 7 minutes, or until steak is browned, stirring occasionally.

2 Add mushrooms and cook 4 to 5 minutes, until tender.

3 Reduce heat to low, stir in gravy, and simmer 10 minutes, or until heated through. Stir in sour cream, and cook 1 to 2 minutes. Serve over warm noodles.

Note:

Top each serving with an additional dollop of sour cream.

Lighter Comfort:

Watching what you're eating? Why not replace the butter with olive oil, the sour cream with a reduced-fat variety, use no-yolk noodles in place of traditional ones, and substitute the regular gravy with a lower-fat option. These little substitutions could save you more than 34 calories, 8 grams fat, and 41 mg sodium per serving.

two-step swiss steak

serves 4 to 6

1-1/2 pounds beef cubed steaks

1/2 teaspoon salt

1/2 teaspoon black pepper

1/2 cup all-purpose flour

3 tablespoons vegetable oil

1 onion, chopped

1 (14-ounce) can Italian-style diced tomatoes, undrained

1 (8-ounce) can tomato sauce

1 tablespoon chopped fresh parsley

2 teaspoons chopped garlic

1 Season the cubed steaks with salt and pepper. Dip the steaks in the flour, coating completely. Heat oil in a large skillet over medium-high heat. Sear the steaks, half at a time, and cook 2 to 3 minutes per side, or until browned. Remove steaks to a platter and brown remaining steaks.

2 Return all steaks to skillet and add remaining ingredients. Cook over low heat 18 to 20 minutes, or until sauce is thickened and meat is tender, stirring occasionally. Serve steaks topped with sauce from pan.

Note:

When you're at the market, don't forget to pick up some curly egg noodles to serve with these.

The secret to keeping the cubed steaks flavorful and moist is to sear them. Just a couple minutes in a hot skillet on both sides seals in their juices. Also, we've found that the heavier skillets are best for maintaining a high temperature, which gives us the best browning.

weeknight salisbury steak

serves 4 to 6

1-1/2 pounds ground chuck

1/4 cup diced onions

1/2 cup Italian bread crumbs

1 egg

1 teaspoon garlic powder

1/2 teaspoon salt

1/2 teaspoon black pepper

1/2 pound fresh mushrooms, sliced

2 (12-ounce) jars beef gravy

1 Preheat oven to 375°F. Coat a 9" x 13" baking dish with cooking spray.

2 In a large bowl, combine ground chuck, onions, bread crumbs, egg, garlic powder, salt, and pepper; mix well.

3 Form into 6 oval patties and place in prepared baking dish. In a medium bowl, combine mushrooms and gravy then pour over patties.

4 Bake, uncovered, 40 to 45 minutes, or until no pink remains.

Note:

For the ultimate taste of comfort, make sure you serve this with a heaping helping of Ultimate Mashed Potatoes (see recipe on page 120).

Did You Know?

Salisbury steak was one of the first main dishes to become a TV dinner favorite in the early 1950s. It's still as popular today so, as easy as it is to make from scratch right at home, why not give it a try?

fall-off-the-bone spareribs

serves 4 to 6

2 cups water

2 cups ketchup

1/2 cup packed dark brown sugar

1/2 onion, chopped

2 tablespoons prepared yellow mustard

2 teaspoons hot pepper sauce

2 teaspoons Worcestershire sauce

5-1/2 pounds pork spareribs

1 In a large saucepan, combine all ingredients except ribs and bring to a boil over high heat, stirring frequently.

2 Reduce heat to medium-low and cook, stirring frequently, 35 to 40 minutes, or until sauce is thick and glossy.

3 Meanwhile, place spareribs in a large pot and add just enough water to cover them; boil ribs over medium-high heat about 30 minutes, or until fork-tender.

4 Preheat oven to 375°F. Place ribs in a large roasting pan and baste heavily with sauce.

5 Bake 30 minutes, basting ribs occasionally and turning once after 15 minutes. Remove ribs from pan and cut apart every 2 or 3 ribs for easier eating. Serve with remaining sauce.

Readers Share Memories:
"Eating ooey gooey ribs is always a memorable experience for our family. It seems the messier they are and the more napkins we use, the better they taste!"
— Randy W., Plano, TX

smothered pork chops

serves 4

1/2 cup all-purpose flour

1/4 teaspoon garlic powder

4 pork loin chops (1-1/2 to
2 pounds total)

2 tablespoons vegetable oil

1 (10-3/4-ounce) can condensed
cream of mushroom soup

1 (8-ounce) can mushroom stems
and pieces, drained

3/4 cup milk

1 (2.8-ounce) container
French-fried onions

1. In a shallow dish, combine flour and garlic powder; mix well. Coat pork chops completely with seasoned flour.

2. In a large skillet, heat oil, then brown pork chops over high heat 2 to 3 minutes per side. Add soup, mushrooms, and milk; mix well and bring to a boil.

3. Reduce heat to medium, cover, and cook 15 to 18 minutes, or until pork chops are cooked through and tender. Sprinkle with onions, and serve.

Serving Suggestion:

We recommend teaming this cozy dish with curly egg noodles to sop up all the sauce. That way, you won't miss a drop of the awesome flavor.

apricot dijon pork chops

serves 6

1/2 teaspoon salt

1/2 teaspoon black pepper

6 boneless pork chops
(1-1/2 pounds total)

1 tablespoon vegetable oil

3 cups chicken broth

3/4 cup apricot preserves

1 tablespoon Dijon-style
mustard

2 cups uncooked instant
white rice

2 tablespoons diced red
bell pepper

1 Sprinkle salt and black pepper evenly over both sides of pork chops.

2 In a large skillet, heat oil over medium-high heat then brown pork chops about 2 to 3 minutes on each side. Remove chops to a plate.

3 Add broth, preserves, and mustard to skillet; mix well and bring to a boil. Stir in rice and bell pepper, reduce heat to low, and place pork chops back in skillet.

4 Cover and cook 8 to 10 minutes, or until pork is cooked to medium or to desired doneness, and rice is tender. Serve immediately.

Did You Know?

Today's pork is very lean and shouldn't be overcooked. According to the Pork Council, the best test of doneness is to use an instant-read meat thermometer to check its internal temperature. They recommend cooking pork chops, roasts, and tenderloins to 160°F, which leaves the center pink and juicy.

battered fish fry

serves 4

1-1/2 cups all-purpose flour

1-1/2 teaspoons baking powder

2 teaspoons sugar

2 teaspoons salt

1 cup water

1 egg

Peanut oil for frying (see Note)

2-1/2 pounds cod fillets or other white-fleshed fish, cut into individual portions

1 In a large bowl, combine flour, baking powder, sugar, salt, water, and egg; mix well.

2 In a large deep skillet, heat 1 inch of oil over medium heat, until hot but not smoking.

3 Dip fish into batter, coating completely, then fry 4 to 5 minutes per side, or until coating is golden and fish flakes easily with a fork.

4 Drain on a paper towel-lined platter. Serve immediately with our Zippy Tartar Sauce (below).

Note:

We recommend only using peanut oil here due to its high tolerance to heat.

Just a Thought:

Many of us have fond memories of a good old-fashioned fish fry. Wherever the fish fry shack was, the lines were long, the fish was steaming hot and the breading was super crunchy. With the heavenly coleslaw and French fries served alongside that fish fry, it's no wonder we'll never forget it.

zippy tartar sauce

makes about 2 cups

1 cup mayonnaise

3/4 cup sweet pickle relish

1/4 cup finely chopped sweet onion

Juice of 1/2 lemon

1 In a small bowl, combine mayonnaise, relish, and onion; mix well. Add lemon juice and stir until well combined. Serve immediately, or cover and chill until ready to use.

salmon croquettes

serves 4

2 (14-3/4-ounce) cans pink or red salmon, drained, boned, and flaked

4 eggs, beaten

2/3 cup instant mashed potato flakes

2 tablespoons finely chopped fresh parsley

1/2 small onion, finely chopped

1/4 teaspoon salt

1/2 teaspoon black pepper

1/4 cup plain bread crumbs

4 tablespoons (1/2 stick) butter

1 In a large bowl, combine all ingredients except bread crumbs and butter; mix well then shape into 12 (1/2-inch-thick) round patties.

2 Place bread crumbs in a shallow dish. Coat each patty completely with the bread crumbs.

3 In a large skillet, heat 2 tablespoons butter over medium heat and cook patties in batches 4 to 5 minutes per side, or until golden, adding more butter as needed. Serve immediately, or make ahead and re-warm in a low oven just before serving.

Serving Suggestion:
Our favorite way to enjoy these is to serve them with our Easy Dill Sauce (below).

easy dill sauce

makes about 1–1/2 cups

1 cup sour cream

1/2 cup mayonnaise

1 tablespoon sweet pickle relish

2 teaspoons lemon juice

1 teaspoon dried dillweed

1 In a small bowl, combine all ingredients; mix until well blended. Serve immediately, or cover and chill until ready to use.

cheeseburger pizza

makes 1 pie, 6 to 8 slices

1 (12- to 14-inch) prepared
   pizza shell

1/2 pound ground beef

1 small onion, chopped

2 teaspoons chopped garlic

1/2 cup ketchup

1/2 teaspoon prepared yellow mustard

1/4 teaspoon salt

1/4 teaspoon black pepper

1/4 cup coarsely chopped dill pickles

1 cup (4 ounces) shredded
   Cheddar cheese

1 Preheat oven to 400°F. Place pizza shell on a pizza pan.

2 In a medium skillet, brown ground beef, onion, and garlic over medium-high heat 4 to 5 minutes, or until no pink remains in beef. Remove from heat and drain off excess liquid.

3 Add ketchup, mustard, salt, and pepper; mix well. Spread beef mixture evenly over pizza shell. Sprinkle with pickles and top with cheese.

4 Bake 10 to 12 minutes, or until crust is crisp and cheese is melted.

Just a Thought:

Take two of the most popular comfort foods, put 'em together and what do you get? A family favorite that will please everyone at the same time.

chicago deep-dish pizza

makes 1 pie, 6 to 8 slices

1 pound hot Italian sausage, casing removed (see Options)

1 pound store-bought pizza dough

1 cup pizza or spaghetti sauce

25 slices pepperoni

1 small green bell pepper, cut into 1/4-inch strips

1 small onion, sliced

1-1/2 cups (6 ounces) shredded mozzarella cheese

1. In a large skillet, cook sausage over medium heat 6 to 8 minutes, or until crumbly and no pink remains, stirring constantly; drain.

2. Preheat oven to 450°F. Coat a 12-inch deep-dish pizza pan with cooking spray. Using your fingertips or the heel of your hand, spread dough so that it covers bottom of pan and comes 3/4 of the way up sides; set aside.

3. Spread sauce over dough then top with sausage, pepperoni, bell pepper, and onion. Sprinkle with cheese.

4. Bake 20 to 25 minutes, or until crust is crisp and golden. Let sit 5 minutes then slice and serve.

Options:

If you prefer a less-spicy pizza, go ahead and use a mild or sweet sausage.

Readers Share Memories:
"I remember the first time I had Chicago-style pizza. I was in Chicago visiting a bunch of friends in college and it was cold. Really cold, and windy. We went to this little dive that had the most amazing pizza. It really warmed us up. Every time I eat it now, I think back to that weekend and my college friends."
— Janie M., St. Louis, MO

crispy crunchy fried chicken

serves 4

1 (3- to 3-1/2-pound) chicken, cut into 8 pieces

2 cups biscuit baking mix

1 teaspoon garlic powder

1 tablespoon salt

2 teaspoons black pepper

1 cup buttermilk

2 tablespoons hot sauce

2 cups vegetable oil

1 Place chicken in a large bowl of ice water and let sit 30 minutes.

2 In a second large bowl, combine baking mix, garlic powder, salt, and pepper; mix well. In a third large bowl, mix buttermilk and hot sauce.

3 Remove chicken from water, shaking off excess water, and dip in seasoned baking mix then into buttermilk mixture, and again in seasoned baking mix, coating completely each time.

4 In a large deep skillet, heat oil over medium-low heat until hot but not smoking. Fry coated chicken in batches for 10 to 12 minutes per side, until golden and no pink remains. Drain on a paper towel-lined platter. Serve immediately.

Note:

Drizzle a bit of honey over the chicken right before serving to make this even more down-home tasty.

Did You Know?

To ensure that you get a really crispy coating, always soak your chicken in ice water before breading or battering it. After all, the best part of fried chicken is the crunch.

dad's bbq chicken

serves 4 to 5

1 (3- to 3-1/2-pound) chicken, cut into 8 pieces

1/2 teaspoon salt

1/2 teaspoon black pepper

1 cup barbecue sauce

1 cup honey

1 chipotle pepper in sauce, finely chopped

1 Preheat oven to 375°F. Coat a rimmed baking sheet with cooking spray.

2 Place chicken on baking sheet and sprinkle evenly with salt and black pepper on both sides. Cook 45 to 55 minutes, or until no pink remains.

3 Preheat grill to medium heat. In a medium bowl, combine remaining ingredients; mix well. Brush chicken with barbecue sauce mixture and grill 5 minutes. Turn chicken, brushing again with sauce, and grill 5 more minutes, or until no pink remains and juices run clear.

Note:
Weather not cooperating or just don't want to use the grill? No problem! Simply slather this sauce on the baked chicken and place under the broiler for a few minutes, just until it begins to caramelize.

Readers Share Memories:
"One of the best memories of my Dad is when he makes what he calls his 'famous honey BBQ chicken' on the grill. He always pre-cooks it in the oven and finishes it off on the grill to make sure it's cooked through and through without burning the outside. I can taste it right now as I write this!"
— Shane R., Lake Mary, FL

simple roasted chicken

serves 4 to 5

2 tablespoons vegetable oil

1 teaspoon paprika

1 teaspoon onion powder

1 teaspoon garlic powder

1 teaspoon salt

1/2 teaspoon black pepper

1 (3-1/2- to 4-pound) chicken

1/2 onion, peeled

4 garlic cloves, peeled

1 Preheat oven to 350°F.

2 In a small bowl, combine oil, paprika, onion powder, garlic powder, salt, and pepper; mix well. Place chicken in a roasting pan and rub with seasoning mixture until completely coated. Place onion and garlic inside chicken cavity.

3 Bake, uncovered, for 1-1/2 hours, or until chicken is no longer pink and juices run clear, using a pastry brush to baste occasionally with pan juices.

Turn this into a one-pot meal by roasting chunks of potatoes, celery, and carrots, all tossed in a bit of oil, salt, and pepper, along with your chicken. You'll save time and cleanup, too.

turkey cacciatore

serves 4 to 6

---

1 tablespoon olive oil

2 bell peppers, thinly sliced

1 large onion, halved and cut into
1/4-inch slices

5 ounces fresh mushrooms, sliced
(about 2 cups)

2 pounds boneless, skinless turkey
breast, cut into 1-inch chunks

1 (26-ounce) jar spaghetti sauce

1/2 cup water

1/4 teaspoon black pepper

1 In a large saucepan, heat oil over medium-high heat. Add bell peppers, onion, and mushrooms, and sauté 4 to 5 minutes, or until tender. Transfer to a bowl, cover and set aside.

2 Add turkey to saucepan and cook about 5 minutes, or until outside of turkey is no longer pink. Return vegetables to saucepan. Stir in spaghetti sauce, water, and black pepper. Reduce heat to medium-low and continue cooking 25 to 30 minutes, or until turkey is tender and cooked through, stirring occasionally.

Note:

You can serve this over warm cooked noodles or pasta for a more complete meal.

Did You Know?

*The word "cacciatore" comes from the Italian word "cacciare", which means "to hunt."
That's why this dish is sometimes also called "Hunter's Stew."*

sensational sandwiches

hot turkey sandwiches

serves 4

2 (12-ounce) jars turkey gravy

3/4 pound deli sliced turkey breast

4 tablespoons (1/2 stick) butter, softened

1 teaspoon rubbed sage

4 slices thick-cut homestyle bread

4 cups prepared mashed potatoes

1 In a large skillet, heat gravy and turkey over medium heat 5 to 7 minutes, or until hot.

2 Meanwhile, in a small bowl, combine butter and sage; mix well. Toast the bread then spread evenly with butter mixture.

3 Top bread with turkey and gravy. Serve with a scoop of warm mashed potatoes and more gravy.

Just a Thought:
The sage butter slathered on the toast gives our sandwich the taste of our Thanksgiving stuffing without all the work. Now that's what we call easy comfort.

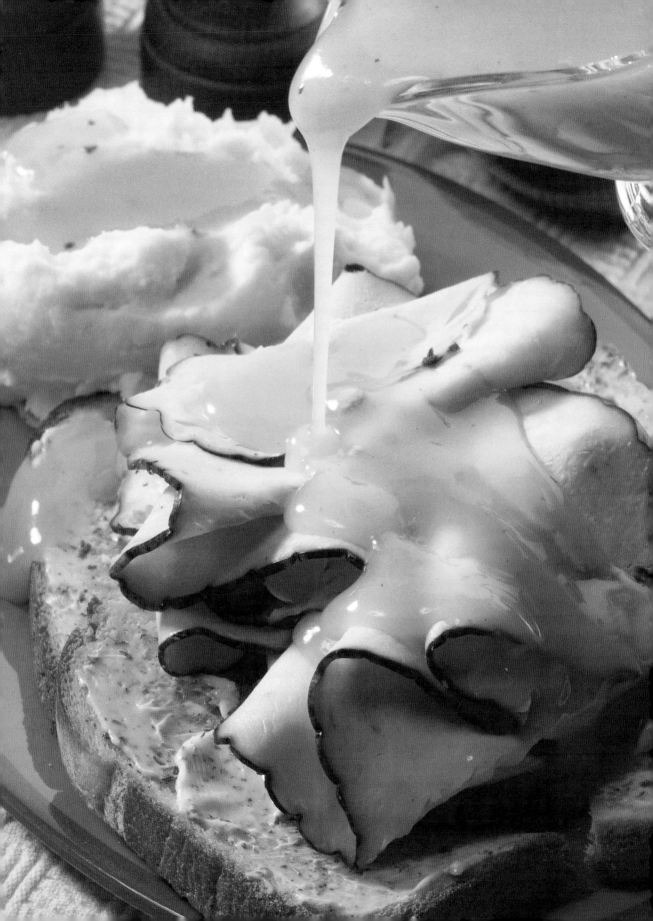

pig on a roll
serves 8

4 pounds boneless pork shoulder or boneless pork butt

1 teaspoon salt

1/2 teaspoon black pepper

1 large onion, chopped

1-1/2 cups root beer soda

1 (28-ounce) bottle barbecue sauce

8 kaiser rolls

1 Place pork in a 6-quart slow cooker and sprinkle with salt and pepper. Top with onions then pour root beer over meat. Cover and cook on high setting 7 to 8 hours, or until pork shreds easily with a fork.

2 Remove pork to a large cutting board and shred with two forks. Place pork mixture in a large skillet. Stir in 1 cup liquid from slow cooker along with onions. Add barbecue sauce; mix well.

3 Cover and heat over medium heat 6 to 8 minutes, or until heated through. Serve on toasted rolls.

Just a Thought:
Our version of a pulled pork sandwich would seem naked without topping it with a hearty helping of our 2-Minute Slaw. So go ahead and pile it on! (See recipe on page 138.)

monte cristo sandwiches

serves 8

6 eggs

1/2 cup milk

1/2 pound thinly sliced deli turkey breast

1/2 pound thinly sliced deli ham

8 (1-ounce) slices Swiss cheese

16 slices egg bread (challah)

4 tablespoons (1/2 stick) butter

1 In a medium bowl, whisk eggs and milk until well combined.

2 Equally divide the turkey, ham, and Swiss cheese on 8 slices of bread. Top with the remaining 8 slices of bread.

3 In a large skillet, melt 1 tablespoon butter over medium heat. Dip two sandwiches, one at a time, in egg mixture, coating completely. Place in skillet and cook 2 to 3 minutes on each side, or until bread is golden and cheese is melted. Remove to a platter and keep warm.

4 Repeat with remaining sandwiches, adding more butter as needed. Serve sandwiches immediately.

Serving Suggestion:
Our taste-testers suggest topping these with warm whole-berry cranberry sauce or serving it on the side for dipping.

fancy-schmancy tuna melts

serves 4

1 (12-ounce) can tuna,
  drained and flaked

1/2 cup mayonnaise

1 celery stalk, sliced

1/4 teaspoon onion powder

1/4 teaspoon black pepper

4 slices rye or pumpernickel bread

4 slices mozzarella cheese

4 slices Cheddar cheese

1 Preheat oven to 375°F. Coat a 10" x 15" baking sheet with cooking spray.

2 In a medium bowl, combine tuna, mayonnaise, celery, onion powder, and pepper; mix well. Spread equal amounts of the mixture on each slice of bread and top each with a slice of mozzarella then a slice of Cheddar cheese.

3 Place on prepared baking sheet and bake 10 minutes, or until cheese is melted. Serve immediately.

Just a Thought:

For many of us, when we hear the words "tuna melt," it instantly brings back memories of the lunch counter at Woolworth's. Ah, those Tuna Melts!

philly cheese steak sandwiches

serves 4

---

3 tablespoons vegetable oil

2 large green bell peppers,
  cut into 1/4-inch strips

2 large onions, thinly sliced

1-1/4 pounds beef top round,
  thinly sliced (see Tip)

1/2 teaspoon black pepper

4 hoagie rolls, split

1 cup processed cheese spread,
  melted (see Note)

1 In a large skillet, heat oil over medium-high heat. Add bell peppers, and sauté 10 minutes. Add onions, and sauté 5 to 7 minutes, or until onions are tender. Transfer to a bowl, cover, and set aside.

2 Add beef to skillet and sprinkle with black pepper; sauté 3 to 5 minutes, or until no pink remains. Return peppers and onions to skillet and cook 2 to 3 minutes, or until heated through.

3 Place mixture over hoagie rolls, drizzle with melted cheese, and serve immediately.

Note:

In Philadelphia, authentic cheese steaks are always topped with Cheeze Whiz. It's an unmistakable taste!

The easiest way to get thinly sliced beef top round is to partially freeze the meat and slice it with an electric knife or, better yet, ask the butcher at the supermarket to do it for you. For this recipe, the thinner the better.

open-faced reuben sandwiches

serves 4

1/2 cup mayonnaise

2 tablespoons ketchup

2 tablespoons sweet pickle relish

1/8 teaspoon garlic powder

1/8 teaspoon salt

1/8 teaspoon black pepper

8 slices rye bread

1 pound sliced deli corned beef

2 (14-1/2-ounce) cans sauerkraut, rinsed and well drained

8 (1-ounce) slices Swiss cheese

1 Preheat oven to 450°F. In a medium bowl, combine mayonnaise, ketchup, relish, garlic powder, salt, and pepper; mix well.

2 Arrange bread on two baking sheets. Spread dressing mixture on each slice (see Serving Suggestion). Top each with an equal amount of corned beef and sauerkraut then a slice of Swiss cheese.

3 Bake 6 to 8 minutes, or until heated through and cheese is melted.

Serving Suggestion:
You might want to use only half the dressing on the sandwiches before baking, then top each with a dollop of the remaining dressing before serving.

Just a Thought:
Some of the biggest and best delis serve their Reubens open-faced, just like this recipe that a friend shared from his deli in Central New York. It's one of the best Reubens you'll ever taste!

classic meatball subs

serves 4

1 pound ground beef

3/4 cup plain dry bread crumbs

1/2 cup grated Parmesan cheese

1/2 cup water

1/4 cup coarsely chopped
fresh parsley

1 egg

1-1/2 teaspoons garlic powder

1 teaspoon salt

1 teaspoon black pepper

2 (26-ounce) jars spaghetti
sauce

4 hoagie rolls, split

1 In a large bowl, gently combine all ingredients
except sauce and rolls (see Tip); mix well. Form
mixture into 12 meatballs and place in a soup pot.
Add spaghetti sauce and stir gently to mix.

2 Bring to a boil over medium heat then reduce
heat to low, cover loosely, and simmer 25 to 30
minutes, or until meatballs are cooked through.

3 Place 3 meatballs on each roll, spoon on some
sauce, and serve.

*The key to plump,
tender meatballs is not to
over-mix, over-handle or pack the
meat mixture. Treat the ground
beef with a little TLC and you'll
end up with some of the best
meatballs you've ever had.*

thanksgiving on a bun

serves 4

3/4 cup mayonnaise

1/4 teaspoon poultry seasoning

4 hoagie rolls, split

1 pound sliced deli turkey breast

2 cups hot prepared stuffing

1 cup whole-berry cranberry sauce

1 Preheat oven to 350°F.

2 In a small bowl, combine mayonnaise and poultry seasoning; mix well. Spread an equal amount of seasoned mayonnaise on each roll. Top with equal amounts of turkey, stuffing, and cranberry sauce.

3 Place sandwiches in a 9" x 13" pan, cover tightly with aluminum foil, and bake 15 to 20 minutes, or until heated through. Carefully unwrap and serve.

Did You Know:

Americans cook more than 46 million turkeys on Thanksgiving Day alone. Thanksgiving might only come once a year, but there's no reason we can't enjoy the tastes of America's #1 food holiday all year long!

mile-high chicken clubs

serves 4

12 slices white bread, toasted

1/2 cup ranch dressing

1/4 head iceberg lettuce,
   leaves separated

4 boneless, skinless cooked
   chicken cutlets (about 1
   pound) (see Tip)

1 large tomato, cut into 8 slices

8 slices bacon, cooked
   until crisp

16 sandwich toothpicks

1 Spread one side of each piece of toast with ranch dressing. Place 4 slices, dressing-side up, on a cutting board. Top each with a quarter of the lettuce and a chicken cutlet, a second piece of toast, 2 tomato slices, 2 bacon slices, and another piece of toast, dressing-side down.

2 Secure each sandwich with 4 toothpicks then slice each with two diagonal cuts, from corner to corner, into quarters.

3 Arrange each sandwich on a plate, with the points of the sandwiches facing out, and serve.

Here's an easy way to cook chicken cutlets: Season chicken with salt and pepper and sauté in a couple tablespoons of olive oil, or bake it on a sprayed baking sheet in a 350°F oven until no longer pink and juices run clear.

chicken parmigiana melts

serves 6

2 eggs

2 tablespoons olive oil

1-1/2 cups plain bread crumbs

1 teaspoon garlic powder

1 teaspoon salt

1/2 teaspoon black pepper

6 boneless, skinless chicken breast halves, pounded to 1/4-inch thickness

Cooking spray

1-1/2 cups spaghetti sauce

1-1/2 cups shredded mozzarella cheese

6 hoagie rolls, split

1 Preheat oven to 350°F. Coat a baking sheet with cooking spray.

2 In a shallow dish, beat together the eggs and olive oil. Place bread crumbs, garlic powder, salt, and pepper in another shallow dish; mix well.

3 Dip each chicken breast into egg mixture then into bread crumbs, pressing down to coat completely. Place chicken on prepared baking sheet and spray top of chicken with cooking spray.

4 Cook 15 to 20 minutes, or until no pink remains. Place 1/4 cup spaghetti sauce and 1/4 cup shredded mozzarella cheese on each chicken breast and cook 5 more minutes. Serve over toasted hoagie rolls.

Lighter Comfort:

Many of us remember these from when we were kids but, in those days, they were fried, not baked. Baking them cuts about 120 calories and 13g of fat per cutlet, but we still get the same great taste!

grilled pb&m

serves 4

1/2 cup marshmallow crème

8 slices egg bread (challah)

1/4 cup peanut butter

2 tablespoons butter, softened

1 Spread marshmallow crème evenly over 4 slices of bread. Spread peanut butter over remaining 4 slices of bread and make 4 sandwiches. Evenly coat both sides of the sandwiches with butter.

2 In a large skillet, cook sandwiches in batches over medium heat, until golden on both sides and marshmallow begins to ooze. Serve immediately.

If you want to get adventurous, we suggest adding some sliced bananas to the sandwiches. Kids of all ages will love 'em!

ultimate grilled cheese sandwiches

serves 5

3/4 cup mayonnaise

1 (3-ounce) package cream cheese, softened

1 cup (4 ounces) shredded Cheddar cheese

1 cup (4 ounces) shredded mozzarella cheese

1/2 teaspoon garlic powder

10 slices sourdough bread

4 tablespoons (1/2 stick) butter, softened

1 In a medium bowl, beat mayonnaise and cream cheese with an electric mixer until light and fluffy. Stir in Cheddar cheese, mozzarella cheese, and garlic powder; mix well.

2 Spread mixture on 5 slices of bread. Top with remaining bread slices.

3 Spread butter on both sides of sandwiches. In a large skillet, cook sandwiches in batches over medium heat, until golden on both sides and cheese is melted.

Just a Thought:

What makes our grilled cheese sandwich the "Ultimate"? When you pull the bread apart and the cheese oozes out, you'll know!

blue bacon steak burgers

serves 6

2 pounds ground beef

1 (4-ounce) package crumbled blue cheese

1/3 cup real bacon bits

1/2 teaspoon black pepper

2 tablespoons steak sauce

6 kaiser rolls

1 Preheat grill to medium-high heat.

2 In a large bowl, combine all ingredients except the rolls; mix well. Shape mixture into 6 equal patties.

3 Grill patties 8 to 12 minutes, or until cooked to medium or desired doneness beyond that, turning halfway through grilling. Serve on rolls.

Serving Suggestion:

Our taste-testers suggest topping each burger with romaine lettuce and some extra blue cheese crumbles. It makes a great burger even better!

fast-food burgers

serves 4

4 large uncut sesame seed rolls

1 pound ground beef

1 tablespoon butter

1/2 cup Thousand Island dressing

2 cups shredded lettuce

8 slices tomato

4 slices American cheese

1 small onion, finely chopped

8 dill pickle chips

1 Cut each roll horizontally into 3 sections; set aside.

2 Form ground beef into 8 thin patties. Melt butter in a large skillet over medium-low heat and cook patties in batches for 3 to 4 minutes per side, or until no longer pink.

3 Spread half the dressing over the four bottom roll sections then sprinkle with half the lettuce and top each with a tomato slice. Place a hamburger patty on each and top with a slice of cheese. Sprinkle chopped onion over the cheese then top with the center roll sections.

4 Spread remaining dressing over the top of the center roll sections then sprinkle with remaining lettuce and tomato slices. Top each with another hamburger patty, 2 dill pickle slices, and the top roll section. Serve, or wrap in wax paper, then serve.

Just a Thought:

Do your kids think that fast food is comfort food? If so, skip the drive-thru but still make 'em happy with these extra-juicy stacked burgers that you can make at home.

old-fashioned chili dogs

serves 6 to 8

1 pound ground beef

1 cup water

1 (8-ounce) can tomato sauce

2 tablespoons chili powder

1 teaspoon garlic powder

1 teaspoon onion powder

1/2 teaspoon salt

1/2 teaspoon black pepper

6 to 8 hot dogs

6 to 8 hot dog rolls, split

1/2 cup chopped onion

1 cup shredded sharp Cheddar cheese

1 In a large skillet, combine ground beef and water; cook over high heat 5 to 7 minutes, or until meat is browned, stirring occasionally. Add tomato sauce, chili powder, garlic powder, onion powder, salt, and pepper; mix well.

2 Bring to a boil then reduce heat to low and simmer 15 to 20 minutes, or until liquid has cooked down, stirring occasionally.

3 Cook hot dogs in a pot of boiling water 3 to 5 minutes, or until heated through. Place in rolls and top with chili sauce. Sprinkle with onion and Cheddar cheese, and serve immediately.

super sides

country skillet potatoes

serves 4 to 6

6 Idaho russet potatoes,
   thinly sliced

1/2 cup vegetable oil

1 large onion, thinly sliced

1 teaspoon salt

1 teaspoon black pepper

1 Fill a large saucepan 3/4 full with water and bring to a boil over high heat.

2 Add potatoes and cook 10 to 12 minutes, or until fork-tender; drain and set aside.

3 In a large skillet, heat oil over medium-high heat. Add onions, and sauté 5 to 6 minutes, or until they start to brown.

4 Add potatoes, salt, and pepper to skillet; toss gently, and cook 15 to 17 minutes, or until brown, turning occasionally.

Just a Thought:

These potatoes go with just about anything – with eggs for breakfast, with steak for dinner – but most people we asked said they like 'em best just with a squirt of ketchup!

ultimate mashed potatoes

serves 4 to 6

8 Idaho russet potatoes
(about 3 pounds),
cut into large chunks

1/2 cup sour cream

1/4 cup milk

1/4 cup (1/2 stick) butter, softened

1 teaspoon salt

1/2 teaspoon black pepper

1 Place potatoes in a large pot and add enough water to cover them. Bring to a boil over high heat. Reduce heat to medium and cook potatoes 20 to 25 minutes, or until fork-tender; drain well.

2 In a large bowl, combine potatoes, sour cream, milk, butter, salt, and pepper; beat with an electric mixer until smooth and well blended.

To peel or not to peel?
Leaving the skin on potatoes not only adds great taste and texture, it also retains many of the nutrients!

homemade beef gravy

makes about 2-1/2 cups

1/4 cup (1/2 stick) butter

1/3 cup all-purpose flour

2-1/2 cups beef broth

1/4 teaspoon salt

1/4 teaspoon black pepper

1 In a medium saucepan, melt butter over medium heat. Add flour and whisk until smooth. Slowly whisk in the broth, salt, and pepper; continue stirring until mixture comes to a boil and thickens.

loaded cheese fries

serves 6

1 (32-ounce) package frozen
    French fries

3/4 cup processed cheese spread,
    melted

2 tablespoons real bacon bits

1/4 cup sliced scallions

1 Preheat oven to 450°F. Spread French fries evenly on a large rimmed baking sheet.

2 Bake 20 to 25 minutes, or until golden.

3 Mound cooked French fries on a serving platter and top with melted cheese, bacon bits, and scallions. Serve immediately.

Readers Share Memories:

"In college, I ate fries smothered with tons of cheese sauce in the dorm cafeteria. They were a mess but just what I needed at that time to get through some of my tougher classes. It definitely contributed to a few extra pounds back then, but it seemed worth it!"
— Judy D., Salem, OR

cheddar potato casserole

serves 6 to 8

3-1/2 cups water

1/2 cup (1 stick) butter

1 teaspoon salt

1/2 teaspoon black pepper

3-1/2 cups instant potato flakes

1 small onion, finely chopped

1-1/2 cups (6 ounces) shredded sharp Cheddar cheese

1 cup (1/2 pint) heavy cream

1 Preheat oven to 350°F. Coat an 8-inch square baking dish with cooking spray.

2 In a large saucepan, bring water, butter, salt, and pepper to a boil over high heat. Remove saucepan from heat and gently stir in potato flakes and onion until well combined.

3 Spoon potato mixture into prepared baking dish. Sprinkle with cheese then pour cream over the top.

4 Bake 35 to 40 minutes, or until heated through and edges are golden.

Note:

For all of you who are skeptical about using instant potato flakes, go ahead and trust us on this one... you won't be disappointed.

Serving Suggestion:

Here's an idea...after putting our Simple Roasted Chicken (see recipe on page 97) in the oven to roast, throw this together and pop it in the oven, too. What a pair!

crispy sweet potato bake

serves 6 to 8

1 (48-ounce) can sweet
 potatoes, drained
 and mashed

3/4 cup sugar

1/4 cup (1/2 stick) butter, melted

2 eggs

1/2 cup milk

1 teaspoon vanilla extract

1/2 teaspoon salt

1 cup coarsely crushed
 frosted corn flakes

1 Preheat oven to 375°F. Coat a 3-quart casserole dish with cooking spray.

2 In a large bowl, combine all ingredients except corn flakes; mix well. Spoon into prepared casserole dish. Sprinkle corn flakes evenly over potato mixture.

3 Bake 35 to 40 minutes, or until firm and golden.

Canned sweet potatoes and yams are practically interchangeable, and in some parts of the country you can get only one or the other. Either one can be used in this recipe.

blue-ribbon potato salad

serves 12

4 pounds white or red potatoes

5 hard-cooked eggs,
  peeled and chopped

1/2 red bell pepper, diced

3 celery stalks, chopped

1 cup sour cream

1-1/2 cups mayonnaise

1 teaspoon onion powder

1-1/2 teaspoons salt

1 teaspoon black pepper

1 Place potatoes in a large soup pot, cover
with water, and bring to a boil over high heat.
Cook 25 to 30 minutes, or until fork-tender.
Drain and cool slightly.

2 Cut potatoes into chunks and place in a large
bowl. Add egg, bell pepper, and celery;
set aside.

3 In a medium bowl, combine remaining
ingredients; mix well. Pour sour cream
mixture over potatoes and mix until thoroughly
combined. Chill 2 to 3 hours before serving.

Lighter Comfort:

*You can save 46 calories and 5 grams
fat per serving by substituting regular
sour cream and mayonnaise with lighter
versions.*

spicy macaroni and cheese

serves 4

1 (8-ounce) package
elbow macaroni

4 cups (16 ounces) shredded
Mexican cheese blend

1-1/2 cups milk

2 eggs

1/4 teaspoon black pepper

1 (4-1/2-ounce) can chopped
green chilies, drained

1 cup coarsely crushed
corn chips

1 Preheat oven to 350°F. Coat a 2-quart casserole
dish with cooking spray.

2 Cook macaroni according to package directions;
drain and place in a large bowl. Add remaining
ingredients except corn chips; mix well then pour
into prepared casserole dish. Sprinkle with
crushed corn chips.

3 Bake 30 to 35 minutes, or until hot and bubbly,
and top is golden.

Note:

*You can assemble this ahead of time by covering it with
plastic wrap and keeping it in the fridge. Just don't add
the corn chips until you're ready to bake and serve it,
or they'll get soggy.*

Did You Know?

*When we surveyed thousands of people as to what they thought were the most comforting foods,
we weren't too surprised by their responses: mac & cheese, meat loaf, mashed potatoes and chocolate are tops on the list.*

smoky mountain baked beans

serves 6

2 (28-ounce) cans baked beans

1/4 cup ketchup

1 tablespoon yellow mustard

1/4 cup plus 2 teaspoons light brown sugar, divided

3 strips bacon

1 Preheat oven to 350°F. Coat a 2-quart baking dish with cooking spray.

2 In a large bowl, combine beans, ketchup, mustard, and 1/4 cup brown sugar; mix well. Pour into prepared baking dish and top with bacon. Sprinkle remaining brown sugar over bacon.

3 Bake, uncovered, 45 to 55 minutes, or until bubbly and bacon is crisp.

Just a Thought:

Pure and simple, these are the best down-home baked beans ever. Actually, the longer you cook 'em, the better they seem to get.

chili corn bread

serves 8

3 cups cornmeal

1 cup all-purpose flour

2 cups milk

2 eggs

1/4 cup melted butter

1 (4-1/2-ounce) can green chilies, drained

1/4 cup light brown sugar

1 tablespoon baking powder

1 teaspoon salt

1 Preheat oven to 400°F. Coat a 9-inch deep-dish pie plate with cooking spray.

2 In a large bowl, combine all ingredients; mix well. Pour batter into prepared pie plate.

3 Bake 25 to 30 minutes, or until golden and a wooden toothpick inserted in center comes out clean. Let cool 5 to 10 minutes, slice into wedges, and serve warm.

Notes:
For an added treat, slather on the butter and finish this off with a drizzle of honey (see photo on previous page).

Did You Know?
Cornmeal comes in yellow and white but, other than the color, there's no difference in taste or texture. Yellow cornmeal is simply ground yellow corn, while white cornmeal comes from white corn.

steakhouse creamed spinach

serves 4 to 5

1 tablespoon butter

2 (9-ounce) packages frozen chopped spinach, thawed and squeezed dry

1 cup heavy cream

1 cup sour cream

1 teaspoon onion powder

1 teaspoon ground nutmeg

1/2 teaspoon salt

1/2 teaspoon black pepper

1 In a medium saucepan, melt butter over medium heat; add spinach, and stir until heated through.

2 Add remaining ingredients to spinach and cook 4 to 5 minutes, or until heated through, stirring occasionally. Serve immediately.

Lighter Comfort:

This is the creamiest if you make it according to the recipe but, of course, you can lighten it up by replacing the heavy cream with whole milk and the regular sour cream with a reduced-fat variety. That alone will save you about 96 calories and 13 grams fat per serving.

bavarian spaetzle

serves 4 to 6

3 cups all-purpose flour

2 tablespoons chopped parsley or mixed herbs (like dried chives, dill, and basil)

2 teaspoons salt, divided

1/4 teaspoon black pepper

4 eggs, beaten

1-3/4 cups milk

1 In a large bowl, combine flour, parsley, 1 teaspoon salt, and the pepper. Make a well in the center and pour in the beaten eggs and milk; mix by hand just until smooth.

2 Bring a large pot of water to a hard, rolling boil and add remaining salt. With a wide slotted spoon, scoop out a spoonful of batter and shake it lightly over the pot until it breaks into strands that fall into the water. The pieces of batter will almost instantly cook, forming spaetzle.

3 When the spaetzle float to the top of the water, remove them with a clean slotted spoon, and drain on paper towels. Repeat until no batter remains.

Serving Suggestion:
Add spaetzle to any soup to make it homemade-yummy, serve it with any meat or chicken dish, or simply serve warm spaetzle plain, with butter or gravy, or topped with shredded cheese.

memory-making homemade noodles

serves 4 to 6

2-1/2 cups all-purpose flour

2 eggs

1/3 cup milk

1 tablespoon chopped
   fresh parsley

1 teaspoon salt

1/4 cup (1/2 stick) butter

1 In a large bowl, combine all ingredients except butter; mix until a stiff dough forms.

2 On a lightly floured work surface, roll out dough to form a 16" x 20" rectangle. Cut into 1/4" x 5" strips, and allow to sit 15 minutes.

3 Meanwhile, bring a soup pot of water to a boil over high heat. Drop about half the noodles into the boiling water (see Note) and cook 10 to 12 minutes, or until tender, stirring frequently.

4 With a slotted spoon, remove noodles to a colander to drain. Repeat with remaining noodles. Toss with butter and serve immediately.

Note:
Make sure to stir the noodles as you drop them into the boiling water to keep them from sticking together.

Just a Thought:
If you've never made noodles from scratch, are you ever in for a treat! We might not recommend these for every night, but our taste-testers insist they're well worth the effort for those special occasions! Try adding these to our Homemade Chicken Soup (page 30).

black-eyed peas

serves 4 to 6

2 tablespoons butter

1 small onion, chopped

1 (10-1/2-ounce) can condensed chicken broth

1/2 cup water

1 (16-ounce) package frozen black-eyed peas, thawed

1 large tomato, cut into large chunks

1/2 teaspoon salt

1 In a large saucepan, melt butter over medium-high heat; sauté onion 3 to 4 minutes, or until tender. Add remaining ingredients and bring to a boil.

2 Reduce heat to medium-low and cook 45 to 50 minutes, or until tomato has cooked down, forming a sauce, stirring occasionally.

Did You Know?
Eating black-eyed peas on New Year's Day is said to bring good luck and prosperity in the coming year.

italian vegetables

serves 6

2 tablespoons olive oil

1 red bell pepper, cut into
1-inch chunks

1 green bell pepper, cut into
1-inch chunks

1 yellow squash, cut into
1-inch chunks

1 zucchini, cut into
1-inch chunks

1 onion, cut into
1/2-inch chunks

1 teaspoon chopped garlic

1/2 teaspoon salt

1/4 teaspoon black pepper

1 (14.5-ounce) can diced
tomatoes, undrained

1 teaspoon Italian seasoning

1 tablespoon grated
Parmesan cheese

1 In a large skillet, heat oil over medium-high heat. Stir in red and green peppers, yellow squash, zucchini, onion, garlic, salt, and black pepper.

2 Cook 6 to 8 minutes, or until vegetables begin to soften, stirring occasionally. Add tomatoes and Italian seasoning; mix well and cook on low heat 8 to 10 minutes, or until vegetables are tender, stirring occasionally. Sprinkle with Parmesan cheese, and serve.

Sharing Memories:

Patty, our Test Kitchen Director, grew up on this dish. Her Uncle Frank had a farm, and her mom would turn the summer's best veggies into a dish just like this. It sure brings back great memories for her.

rice 'n' broccoli bake

serves 6 to 8

1 (32-ounce) package frozen broccoli florets, thawed and well drained

2 cups cooked rice (see note)

1 (16-ounce) container processed cheese spread

1 (10-3/4-ounce) can condensed cream of mushroom soup

1/2 teaspoon salt

1/2 teaspoon black pepper

1 (2.8-ounce) can French-fried onions

1 Preheat oven to 375°F. Coat a 3-quart casserole dish with cooking spray.

2 In a large bowl, combine all ingredients except French-fried onions; mix well until thoroughly combined. Pour into prepared casserole dish.

3 Cover and bake 45 minutes, or until heated through. Uncover and sprinkle onions evenly over the top; bake 5 to 10 more minutes, or until golden and bubbly.

Serving Suggestion:

How about using cooked brown rice to add some healthy fiber to this dish? Also, if you want to hearty this up and make it a main dish, just add a couple cups of diced, cooked rotisserie chicken and you'll have an all-in-one meal with only one bowl to wash...now that's comforting!

scalloped brussels sprouts

serves 4 to 5

- 1 (10-3/4-ounce) can condensed cream of mushroom soup
- 1/2 cup milk
- 1/4 teaspoon black pepper
- 1 (16-ounce) package frozen Brussels sprouts, thawed
- 2 tablespoons bacon bits

1 In a large skillet, combine soup, milk, and pepper. Heat over medium heat for 5 minutes, stirring occasionally.

2 Stir in Brussels sprouts; simmer over low heat 10 minutes, or until hot. Sprinkle with bacon bits, and serve.

Did You Know?

Brussels sprouts got their name due to the fact that they were widely cultivated around Brussels, Belgium, during the early 16th century. Today, Brussels sprouts are available around the world, and people seem to have strong feelings for them – they either love them or dislike them intensely. Who would think a little veggie could be so controversial?

golden corn pudding

serves 4 to 6

1 (17-ounce) can whole-kernel corn, drained

1 (16-1/2-ounce) can cream-style corn

1/4 cup milk

1/4 cup sugar

2 eggs, beaten

2 tablespoons cornstarch

1-1/2 cups crushed butter crackers, divided

1 Preheat oven to 350°F. Coat a 1-1/2-quart casserole dish with cooking spray.

2 In a large bowl, combine all ingredients except 1/2 cup crushed crackers; mix well. Spoon mixture into prepared casserole dish.

3 Sprinkle with remaining crushed crackers and bake 45 to 50 minutes, or until golden and set. Serve immediately.

Just a Thought:

Why is it we make certain dishes that we love only for Thanksgiving and then put the recipe away until the next year? Well, this is one of those traditional recipes that's so good yet so easy you should plan on making it on a regular basis.

fried green tomatoes

serves 6 to 8

---

1 egg

1/4 cup water

1-1/2 teaspoons salt

1/2 teaspoon black pepper

5 green tomatoes, cored and cut into 1/4-inch slices (see Tip)

1 cup all-purpose flour

1 cup self-rising white cornmeal mix

1-1/2 cups vegetable oil

1 In a large bowl, combine egg, water, salt, and pepper; mix well. Add tomato slices and toss to coat well.

2 In a shallow dish, combine flour and cornmeal mix; mix well. Dip each tomato slice into flour mixture, coating completely, then place on a baking sheet. Repeat until all slices are coated.

3 In a large skillet, heat oil over high heat until hot but not smoking. Reduce heat as needed. Fry a few tomato slices at a time for 2 to 3 minutes per side, or until golden. Drain on a paper towel-lined platter and keep warm until all are cooked. Serve warm.

Green tomatoes are most commonly available in early summer throughout most of the country, but with their popularity growing, you can often find them during the rest of the year. Keep an eye out for them and grab them when you can.

2-minute slaw

serves 6

1 cup mayonnaise

1/4 cup apple cider vinegar

1/4 cup sugar

1/2 teaspoon salt

1/4 teaspoon black pepper

6 cups (1 small head) shredded cabbage (see Note)

1 cup (about 2 large) shredded carrots (see Note)

1 In a large bowl, combine mayonnaise, vinegar, sugar, salt, and pepper. Add shredded cabbage and carrots; toss to coat well. Serve immediately.

Note:

To make this even easier, you can use 2 (10-ounce) packages of pre-shredded coleslaw mix instead of cutting the cabbage and carrots by hand.

Did You Know?

Hippocrates, the father of modern medicine, realized the medicinal value of apple cider vinegar, and often prescribed it for its healing properties.

memorable desserts

peanut butter cup cheesecake

serves 12

20 cream-filled chocolate sandwich cookies

4 tablespoons (1/2 stick) butter, melted

3 (8-ounce) packages cream cheese, softened

1 cup sugar

4 eggs

1 cup peanut butter

1 teaspoon vanilla extract

1-1/2 cups coarsely chopped peanut butter cup candies, divided

1 cup dark chocolate chips

1 Preheat oven to 350°F.

2 Place cookies in a resealable plastic storage bag and finely crush, using a rolling pin. Place in a medium bowl and add butter; mix well then spread over bottom of a 10-inch springform pan. Chill until ready to use.

3 In a large bowl, combine cream cheese and sugar; beat with an electric mixer on low speed until creamy. Beat in eggs, one at a time, then add peanut butter and vanilla; mix well. With a spoon, stir in 1 cup peanut butter cup candies then pour into pan.

4 Bake 55 to 60 minutes, until firm in center; cake will crack slightly. Remove from oven and let cool.

5 Melt chocolate chips in a microwave-safe bowl for 60 to 90 seconds, stirring occasionally until smooth. Place in resealable plastic storage bag, cut tip off 1 corner of bag, and drizzle chocolate over cheesecake. Sprinkle with remaining peanut butter candies. Refrigerate 6 to 8 hours, or overnight. Remove from springform pan then serve.

Just a Thought:

This grown-up cheesecake is made from favorite childhood ingredients. Just try not to eat them all before the cake is assembled!

southern peach cobbler

serves 8

1 cup sugar

2 tablespoons cornstarch

1/2 teaspoon ground cinnamon

1/2 cup water

2 (16-ounce) bags frozen peach slices or 8 cups fresh peach slices

Biscuit Topping:

1 cup all-purpose flour

2 tablespoons sugar

1-1/2 teaspoons baking powder

1/4 teaspoon salt

1/4 cup vegetable shortening

1 egg, slightly beaten

1/4 cup milk

1 Preheat oven to 400°F.

2 In a large saucepan, combine 1 cup sugar, the cornstarch, and cinnamon. Add water; stir to combine. Add peach slices and cook on medium-high heat until mixture comes to a boil, stirring occasionally. Simmer 1 minute, stirring constantly.

3 Meanwhile, for biscuit topping, combine flour, 2 tablespoons sugar, the baking powder, and salt. Using a fork or pastry cutter, cut in shortening until coarse crumbs form. Combine egg and milk, and pour into flour mixture; stir just until moistened.

4 Pour peach mixture into a 2-quart baking dish. Drop biscuit mixture in 7 to 8 mounds on top of peaches.

5 Bake 20 minutes, or until golden. Serve warm.

Note:
We think this is best topped with a generous scoop of ice cream or whipped cream.

after-school chocolate cake

serves 12 to 14

1 cup sugar

1/2 cup vegetable shortening

4 eggs

1-1/2 cups chocolate syrup

1-1/4 cups all-purpose flour

1 teaspoon baking powder

1 (16-ounce) can
vanilla frosting

1 Preheat oven to 350°F. Coat a Bundt pan with cooking spray.

2 In a large bowl, cream sugar and shortening with an electric mixer on low speed. Gradually beat in the eggs, one at a time. Slowly mix in the chocolate syrup, flour, and baking powder.

3 Pour into prepared Bundt pan and bake 40 to 45 minutes, or until toothpick inserted in center comes out clean.

4 Let cool 10 minutes then invert onto serving platter. Cool completely.

5 Microwave canned frosting without cover (making sure to first remove the entire foil seal) for 30 to 45 seconds, or until pourable. With a spoon, drizzle frosting over cake, allowing it to drip down the sides. Let set before serving.

Just a Thought:

If the kids go to make chocolate milk and can't find the chocolate syrup, chances are Mom made this cake and is hiding it until after dinner.

neighborly banana cake

serves 12 to 15

2 cups all-purpose flour

1 cup sugar

1 teaspoon baking soda

1/2 teaspoon salt

1 cup mashed ripe banana (see Tip)

2/3 cup mayonnaise

1/4 cup water

1-1/2 teaspoons vanilla extract

1/2 cup finely chopped nuts

1 Preheat oven to 350°F. Coat a 9" x 13" baking dish with cooking spray.

2 In a large bowl, mix together flour, sugar, baking soda, and salt. Add mashed banana, mayonnaise, water, and vanilla; mix until well combined. Stir in nuts then pour into prepared baking dish.

3 Bake 25 to 30 minutes, or until toothpick inserted in center comes out clean. Let cool then cut into squares.

Note:

For a fancier treat, add 1/2 cup chocolate chips to batter and frost it with a canned cream cheese or chocolate frosting.

If you have some bananas that are a bit too ripe to eat, this is a perfect way to use them. Also, you might think that mayonnaise is a strange ingredient to include in a cake, but it's a great substitute for eggs and oil and produces a very moist texture.

blueberry pound cake

serves 12

1/2 pound (2 sticks) butter, softened

1-1/2 cups granulated sugar

3 eggs

2 cups plus 1 tablespoon all-purpose flour, divided

1/3 cup milk

1 teaspoon vanilla extract

1 cup fresh or frozen and thawed blueberries

Confectioners' sugar for garnish

1 Preheat oven to 300°F. Grease and flour a 9" x 5" loaf pan.

2 In a large bowl, cream butter with an electric mixer on medium speed; gradually add granulated sugar, beating until light and fluffy.

3 Add eggs, one at a time, beating after each addition. Gradually add 2 cups flour alternately with milk, beginning and ending with flour and mixing well after each addition. Stir in vanilla and blueberries that have been tossed in the remaining 1 tablespoon flour (see Tip).

4 Pour batter into prepared pan and bake 1 hour and 25 minutes, or until toothpick inserted in center comes out clean. Cool in pan 15 to 20 minutes then remove to a wire rack. Let cool completely then sprinkle with confectioners' sugar.

Tossing the blueberries in flour prevents them from sinking to the bottom of the pan during baking. This trick can also be used when adding ingredients like chocolate chips or raisins to almost any cake. This will help ensure that every bite is full of the same goodness.

pineapple upside-down cake

makes 2 cakes, each serves 6 to 8

2/3 cup packed light
   brown sugar

4 tablespoons (1/2 stick) butter,
   melted

1 (20-ounce) can pineapple
   slices, drained

10 maraschino cherries

1 (18.25-ounce) package
   yellow cake mix

1 cup water

1/4 cup vegetable oil

3 eggs

1. Preheat oven to 350°F. Sprinkle brown sugar evenly over bottom of two 8-inch round cake pans and pour butter evenly over sugar.

2. In each pan, arrange pineapple slices in a single layer over sugar and place a cherry in center of each slice.

3. In a large bowl, combine cake mix, water, oil, and eggs; beat with an electric mixer on low speed until well combined.

4. Evenly divide batter between the two pans and bake 30 to 35 minutes, or until a toothpick inserted in center of each comes out clean. Let cakes stand 5 minutes.

5. Loosen gently with a knife and invert onto 2 platters. Serve warm or allow to cool completely before serving.

Just a Thought:

Since the pineapple is the symbol of hospitality, and this recipe makes 2 cakes, why not enjoy one yourself and share the other with a friend or neighbor?

classic chocolate brownies

serves 12 to 15

1/4 cup water

1-1/2 cups sugar

8 tablespoons (1 stick) butter

3 cups semisweet chocolate chips, divided

4 eggs

1 teaspoon vanilla extract

1-1/2 cups all-purpose flour

1/4 teaspoon salt

1/2 cup chopped walnuts (optional)

1 Preheat oven to 350°F. Coat a 9" x 13" baking pan with cooking spray.

2 In a saucepan, combine water, sugar, and butter. Bring to a boil over medium heat, stirring constantly. Remove from heat, and stir in 2 cups chocolate chips until smooth. Let cool 5 minutes. Add eggs, one at a time, stirring just until blended. Stir in vanilla, flour, and salt; mix well. Stir in remaining chocolate chips and the walnuts, if desired.

3 Spread mixture into prepared baking pan. Bake 25 to 30 minutes, or until toothpick inserted in center comes out clean. Cool in pan on wire rack. Cut into squares.

Serving Suggestion:

For the biggest WOW, why not serve these warm, with a scoop of vanilla ice cream and a drizzle of hot fudge? The contrast of the hot and cold is guaranteed to tantalize your taste buds.

bakery crumb cake

serves 15 to 18

2 cups all-purpose flour

1 cup granulated sugar

2 teaspoons baking powder

1/4 teaspoon salt

4 tablespoons (1/2 stick) butter, softened

3/4 cup milk

1 egg

1 teaspoon vanilla extract

Topping

2 cups all-purpose flour

1 cup granulated sugar

1/2 pound (2 sticks) butter, softened

2 teaspoons ground cinnamon

1 tablespoon confectioners' sugar

1 Preheat oven to 350°F. Coat a 12" x 15" rimmed baking sheet with cooking spray.

2 In a large bowl, combine 2 cups flour, 1 cup granulated sugar, the baking powder, salt, 1/4 cup butter, the milk, egg, and vanilla; mix well. Spread on prepared baking sheet.

3 In a medium bowl, combine topping ingredients except confectioners' sugar, using a fork or pastry cutter, until coarse crumbs form. Evenly sprinkle over batter and bake 25 to 30 minutes, or until a toothpick inserted in center comes out clean. Let cool then sprinkle with confectioners' sugar.

Serving Suggestion:
This recipe is great as is but, for a little novelty, try baking it in muffin tins for individual portions. Just be sure to adjust the cooking time accordingly to about 18 to 20 minutes.

carrot cake squares

serves 12 to 15

2 cups all-purpose flour

2 teaspoons baking soda

1/2 teaspoon salt

2 teaspoons ground cinnamon

3 eggs

3/4 cup buttermilk

3/4 cup vegetable oil

2 cups granulated sugar

2 teaspoons vanilla extract

1 (8-ounce) can crushed
  pineapple, drained

3 cups shredded raw carrots

1 cup ground pecans

Pecan halves for garnish

Cream Cheese Frosting
  1 (8-ounce) package cream
    cheese, softened

  3 tablespoons butter, softened

  1 teaspoon vanilla extract

  1 cup confectioners' sugar

1 Preheat oven to 350°F. Coat a 9" x 13" baking dish with cooking spray.

2 In a medium bowl, combine flour, baking soda, salt, and cinnamon; mix well and set aside.

3 In a large bowl, combine eggs, buttermilk, oil, granulated sugar, and 2 teaspoons vanilla; beat with an electric mixer on low speed. Add pineapple, carrots, and pecans; mix well. Beat in flour mixture until well combined then pour into prepared baking dish.

4 Bake 35 to 40 minutes, or until toothpick inserted in center comes out clean. Let cool.

5 In a medium bowl, combine frosting ingredients except confectioners' sugar. Slowly mix in confectioners' sugar until smooth and creamy. Frost the cooled cake, cut into squares, and garnish each square with a pecan half.

Readers Share Memories:

"I'm not a big chocolate-lover so, every year when I was growing up, my Mom would make me a carrot cake as my birthday cake. Now that I'm grown up, I make it for myself several times a year and, every time, I think back to those family birthday get-togethers."
— Barbara L., Youngstown, OH

oatmeal raisin cookies

makes about 4 dozen

1-1/2 cups all-purpose flour

1 teaspoon baking soda

1 teaspoon ground cinnamon

1/2 pound (2 sticks) butter, softened

1 cup packed light brown sugar

1/2 cup granulated sugar

2 eggs

1 teaspoon vanilla extract

3 cups quick oats, uncooked

1 cup raisins

1 Preheat oven to 350°F. In a medium bowl, combine flour, baking soda, and cinnamon; mix well.

2 In a large bowl, combine butter, brown sugar, and granulated sugar; beat with an electric mixer on low speed until creamy. Add eggs and vanilla; mix well. Add flour mixture; mix well. Stir in oats and raisins; mix well.

3 Drop dough by rounded tablespoonfuls onto ungreased baking sheets and bake 10 to 12 minutes, or until light golden. Cool 1 minute on baking sheets; remove to wire rack to cool completely.

Lighter Comfort:

One key to lightening up any dessert is eating it in moderation, and with these Oatmeal Raisin Cookies, that's easy if you have just one cookie at a time. Plus, you're getting all the health benefits of oatmeal, too.

colossal chocolate chunk cookies

makes about 1-1/2 dozen

2 cups all-purpose flour

1/2 teaspoon baking soda

1/2 teaspoon salt

3/4 cup (1-1/2 sticks) butter, melted

1 cup packed light brown sugar

1/2 cup granulated sugar

1 tablespoon vanilla extract

1 egg

1 egg yolk

2 cups semisweet chocolate chunks

1 Preheat oven to 325°F. Coat baking sheets with cooking spray.

2 In a medium bowl, mix together flour, baking soda, and salt; set aside.

3 In a large bowl, combine melted butter, brown sugar, and granulated sugar; beat with an electric mixer on low speed until well blended. Beat in vanilla, egg, and egg yolk until light and creamy. Mix in the dry ingredients until just blended. With a spoon, stir in the chocolate chunks.

4 Drop cookie dough 1/4 cup at a time onto the prepared baking sheets, about 3 inches apart.

5 Bake 15 to 17 minutes, or until edges are light golden. Cool on baking sheets 3 to 5 minutes then remove to wire racks to cool completely.

Just a Thought:

Better make an extra batch of these cookie jar favorites, 'cause they'll be gone in a flash!

strawberry pretzel bars

serves 12

2 cups finely crushed pretzels

3/4 cup (1-1/2 sticks) butter, melted

1 cup plus 3 tablespoons sugar, divided

2 (4-serving) packages strawberry-flavored gelatin

2 cups boiling water

1 (16-ounce) package frozen strawberries (see Note)

1 (8-ounce) package cream cheese, softened

1 (12-ounce) container frozen whipped topping, thawed

1 Preheat oven to 400°F. Coat a 9" x 13" baking dish with cooking spray.

2 In a medium bowl, combine crushed pretzels, melted butter, and 3 tablespoons sugar. Press mixture into bottom of prepared baking dish. Bake 8 minutes; let cool.

3 In a large bowl, dissolve gelatin in boiling water. Add strawberries and chill until slightly thickened.

4 In another large bowl, combine cream cheese and remaining sugar; beat with an electric mixer on low speed until smooth and creamy. Fold in whipped topping and spread evenly over pretzel crust.

5 Beat gelatin and strawberries until berries are broken up. Spread over cream cheese layer. Cover and chill at least 4 hours, or until firm.

Note:

Although the strawberries need to be thawed slightly so that they're not frozen solid, the colder they are, the faster the gelatin will thicken.

drop-in ice cream sandwiches

serves 12

1 (16-ounce) package
chocolate sandwich cookies,
crushed (about 3 cups)

1/3 cup butter, melted

1/2 gallon vanilla ice cream,
slightly softened

1 Line a 9" x 13" baking pan with aluminum foil.

2 Crush the cookies in a food processor or by
placing in a resealable plastic storage bag and
crushing with a rolling pin. Add melted butter;
mix well.

3 Press half the cookie mixture firmly into
prepared baking pan. Spread softened ice cream
over cookie mixture then press remaining cookie
mixture gently on top of ice cream. Cover and
freeze at least 6 hours.

4 Cut into 12 sandwich squares.

Just a Thought:

*These get their name from when guests would "drop in" unexpectedly. While that doesn't
happen as often these days, they're still good to have on hand for anytime you want 'em or when
friends do "drop in."*

sinful chocolate sherbet

makes about 1 quart

3/4 cup sugar

1/2 cup unsweetened cocoa

1/2 cup hot water

2 cups milk

1/4 cup cold water

1 In a small saucepan, combine sugar and cocoa. Place over low heat and slowly stir in hot water. Continue stirring 2 to 3 minutes, or until sugar is dissolved and cocoa is thoroughly blended.

2 Remove from heat and gradually stir in milk. Pour into a 9" x 13" baking dish, cover, and freeze 3 to 4 hours, or until firm.

3 Break up frozen mixture and place in bowl of a food processor that has been fitted with its metal cutting blade, or a blender. Add cold water and process 2 to 3 minutes, or until smooth and light-colored.

4 Pour into an airtight storage container. Seal and freeze at least 2 hours, or until firm.

Lighter Comfort:

For a lower-fat sherbet, use low-fat milk instead of whole milk.

old-time diner gelatin parfaits

serves 8

1 (4-serving) package cherry-flavored gelatin, mixed according to package directions

1 (4-serving) package lime-flavored gelatin

1 cup boiling water

1-1/2 cups ice cubes, divided

1/2 cup sour cream

1 (8-ounce) can pineapple tidbits, drained

1 (5.5-ounce) can apricot nectar

1 (4-serving) package orange- or peach-flavored gelatin

1 Pour cherry gelatin equally into 8 large parfait glasses. Chill 2 hours, or until set.

2 In a large bowl, dissolve lime gelatin in boiling water. Add 1/2 cup ice cubes and mix until cubes are melted and gelatin is slightly thickened. With an electric mixer on low speed, beat in sour cream. Fold in pineapple tidbits and layer evenly over cherry gelatin. Chill 2 hours, or until set.

3 In a small saucepan, bring apricot nectar to a boil over medium-high heat.

4 In a medium bowl, dissolve orange gelatin in boiling apricot nectar. Add remaining ice cubes and stir until melted. Spoon over lime gelatin layer in each parfait glass then cover and chill at least 3 hours, or until firm.

Note:

For a fruit-packed parfait, add drained canned apricot halves to the final layer.

Just a Thought:

The eye-catching colorful layers of this yummy diner dessert will remind you of simpler times.

double-chocolate cream pie

serves 6

1 refrigerated rolled pie crust
(from a 15-ounce package)

2/3 cup granulated sugar

1/4 cup unsweetened cocoa

3 tablespoons cornstarch

1/4 teaspoon salt

2 cups cold milk

1/4 cup chocolate syrup

1 teaspoon vanilla extract

1 (12-ounce) container frozen
whipped topping, thawed

1 Unroll pie crust and place in a 9-inch deep-dish pie plate, pressing crust firmly into plate; flute, if desired. Bake pie shell according to package directions; let cool.

2 In a medium saucepan, combine sugar, cocoa, cornstarch, and salt. Gradually stir in milk and chocolate syrup. Bring to a boil over medium heat, stirring constantly. Remove from heat and stir in vanilla. Pour into cooled pie crust then chill 1 hour.

3 Spread whipped topping evenly over pie, cover loosely, and chill 8 hours or overnight before serving.

You can make your own whipped cream by combining 1/2 pint (1 cup) heavy cream and 2 tablespoons confectioners' sugar and beating with an electric mixer on low speed until stiff peaks form. To make the pie look extra special, just before serving, top with shaved chocolate or sprinkles.

piled-high apple pie

serves 6

3/4 cup plus 1 teaspoon sugar, divided

1-1/8 teaspoons ground cinnamon, divided

8 medium-sized baking apples, peeled, cored and quartered

2 tablespoons all-purpose flour

1 tablespoon plus 2 teaspoons butter, softened

1 teaspoon lemon juice

1 (15-ounce) package refrigerated rolled pie crusts

1 Preheat oven to 425°F. In a small bowl, combine 1 teaspoon sugar and 1/8 teaspoon cinnamon; mix well and set aside.

2 In a large bowl, combine apples, flour, 1 tablespoon butter, the lemon juice, remaining 3/4 cup sugar, and 1 teaspoon cinnamon; toss to coat apples well.

3 Unroll 1 pie crust and place in a 9-inch deep-dish pie plate, pressing crust firmly against plate. Pour apple mixture into crust then place remaining pie crust over mixture. Trim and pinch edges together to seal, fluting if desired. Using a sharp knife, cut four 1-inch slits in top.

4 Melt remaining butter then brush over top of crust; sprinkle with reserved sugar mixture.

5 Bake 45 to 50 minutes, or until crust is golden.

Note:

Since the pie is piled so high that it may bubble over, we suggest placing a baking sheet under it to make cleanup a breeze.

Selecting the right apple can make the difference between a good apple pie and a great apple pie. When it comes to baking apples, be sure to use a variety that can stand up to heat. We suggest Granny Smith, Golden Delicious or Gala.

strawberry rhubarb pie

serves 6

1 (15-ounce) package refrigerated rolled pie crusts, at room temperature

1 quart strawberries, washed, hulled and quartered

1 cup sugar

1 cup cubed fresh rhubarb (see Note)

1/3 cup all-purpose flour

1 tablespoon butter, melted

1 Preheat oven to 425°F. Unroll one pie crust and place in a 9-inch deep-dish pie plate, pressing crust firmly into plate.

2 In a large bowl, combine strawberries and sugar; mix well until sugar dissolves. Add rhubarb, flour, and butter; mix well and spoon into pie crust.

3 Place remaining pie crust on a work surface and, using the plastic cap of a soda bottle, cut 8 to 10 circles from the center, forming polka dots, leaving a 2-inch border around the edges.

4 Place cut-out crust over strawberry mixture. Trim and pinch edges together to seal, fluting if desired.

5 Bake 30 to 35 minutes, or until crust is golden and filling is bubbly. Allow to cool slightly before serving, or chill until ready to serve.

Note:

If fresh rhubarb is not in season, you can substitute 1 cup frozen rhubarb that's been thawed and drained.

Just a Thought:

Mention strawberry rhubarb pie to a group of friends and you'll always find someone who says it's their absolute favorite! One forkful will be all you need to have this become a favorite in your house, too.

whoopie pies

makes about 18 sandwich pies

1 (18.25-ounce) package devil's food cake mix

3/4 cup water

1/2 cup vegetable oil

3 eggs

1 cup milk

5 tablespoons all-purpose flour

1-1/4 cups sugar

1 cup vegetable shortening

2 teaspoons vanilla extract

1 Preheat oven to 350°F. Coat baking sheets with cooking spray.

2 In a large bowl, combine cake mix, water, oil, and eggs; beat with an electric mixer on low speed until well blended. Drop batter by teaspoonfuls onto prepared baking sheets.

3 Bake 8 to 10 minutes, or until toothpick inserted in center comes out clean. Let cool slightly then remove to a wire rack to cool completely.

4 In a saucepan, combine milk and flour and cook over medium-high heat, stirring constantly until it forms a thick paste; let cool.

5 In a medium bowl, beat sugar and shortening until fluffy; stir in vanilla then add the cooled flour mixture and beat until doubled in volume.

6 Turn half the cooled cakes over on their backs then spoon a dollop of filling onto each. Place remaining cakes on top of the filling, forming sandwiches.

Did You Know?

Whoopie pies originated with the Amish people. It's not uncommon to find roadside stands dotted along their country roads, selling these memory-making treats.

notes

drinks, anyone?

soda fountain root beer float

serves 1

2 scoops vanilla ice cream, divided

1 cup chilled root beer soda

Whipped cream for garnish

Maraschino cherry for garnish

1 Place 1 scoop of ice cream in a tall glass. Pour in half the root beer then add remaining scoop of ice cream and remaining root beer.

2 Top with whipped cream and cherry. Serve immediately.

Headnote:

Make sure you serve this with a straw and a long-handled spoon to help enjoy every last bit of this great flavor combo. (They give it that old-fashioned ice cream fountain look, too!)

rich 'n' creamy chocolate shake

serves 4

6 large scoops chocolate ice cream

2 cups milk

1/4 cup chocolate syrup

1 In a blender, combine all ingredients on high speed until thoroughly mixed. Pour into 4 glasses and serve immediately.

Just a Thought:

Years ago, they had to use a stainless steel cup and a milkshake maker.
Now we can just throw these 3 ingredients in our blender then sip away!

chocolate malted

serves 4

6 large scoops vanilla ice cream

1-1/2 cups milk

2 cups chocolate malted milk balls, crushed (see Tip)

1 In a blender, combine all ingredients and blend on high speed until thoroughly mixed. Pour into tall glasses and serve immediately.

Here's an easy way to crush the malted milk balls: place them in a resealable plastic storage bag, close tightly, and crush with a rolling pin.

Lighter Comfort:

You know, you can use whole milk, 2%, 1%, or skim milk in here – the choice is yours. And if you want to lighten it up, use low-fat frozen yogurt in place of the ice cream.

easy egg cream

serves 1

1/2 cup cold milk

1 cup seltzer or club soda

2 tablespoons chocolate syrup

1 Pour milk into a tall glass. Add seltzer to within 1 inch of glass rim; using a long spoon, stir vigorously. (This will cause it to become white and bubbly, with a good head of foam.)

2 Very gently, pour chocolate syrup slowly down the inside of the glass. Using the long spoon, stir briskly only at the bottom of the glass where the syrup sits (see Note).

Note:
The drink should have a dark brown bottom and a 1-inch pure white foam top. If you mix it too much, the foam will disappear.

Did You Know?
Originating in New York, this famous old-fashioned thirst-quencher known as the egg cream actually contains no eggs and no cream...go figure! Pass out the straws and watch your gang enjoy the pure sipping sensation of our Easy Egg Cream recipe.

pink lemonade slushy

serves 4

3 cups ice cubes

1/2 cup lemon juice
(juice from about 3 large
fresh lemons)

1/2 cup water

1 tablespoon maraschino
cherry juice

1/2 cup sugar

Lemon slices for garnish

1 In a blender, combine all ingredients except lemon slices. Blend on high speed until mixture is slushy.

2 Pour into glasses, top each with a lemon slice, and serve immediately.

Readers Share Memories:
"On hot summer days, my mom used to make us kids lemon slushies to cool off. Now I make them for my kids!"
— Paula T., Lafayette, IN

sunshine smoothie

serves 4

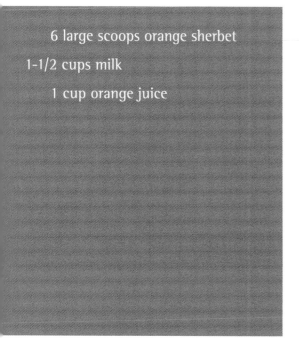

6 large scoops orange sherbet

1-1/2 cups milk

1 cup orange juice

1 In a blender, combine all ingredients on high speed until thoroughly mixed.

2 Pour into glasses and serve immediately.

Just a Thought:

Don't feel guilty about enjoying this smoothie...it's packed with calcium and vitamin C. For an even healthier version, use 1% milk.

sweet iced tea

serves 4 to 6

10 cups water, divided

1/8 teaspoon baking soda (see Tip)

7 tea bags

1-1/2 cups sugar

1 lemon, thinly sliced

Fresh mint leaves for garnish (optional)

1 In a large saucepan, bring 5 cups water to a boil over high heat. Stir in baking soda and tea bags; remove from heat, cover, and let steep 15 minutes.

2 Remove and discard tea bags. Stir in sugar until dissolved. Add remaining 5 cups cold water and the lemon slices. Pour into 1/2-gallon container and refrigerate 2 to 4 hours, or until chilled.

3 Serve over ice in tall glasses, garnished with mint, if desired.

Using baking soda in this recipe is no mistake. It removes any bitterness from the tea, leaving us with a smooth and flavorful drink.

hot cinnamon apple cider

serves 6

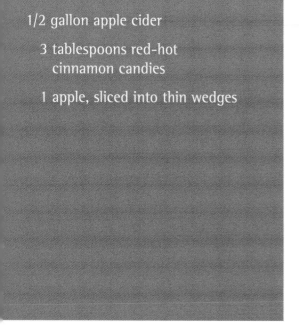

1/2 gallon apple cider

3 tablespoons red-hot cinnamon candies

1 apple, sliced into thin wedges

1 In a large saucepan, combine all ingredients over medium heat. Simmer until hot and the cinnamon candies are melted, stirring occasionally.

2 Pour into mugs and serve warm.

Readers Share Memories:

"I love red-hot cinnamon candies! Even though they almost burn my tongue, they're irresistible!"
— Mike W., Harrisburg, PA

nana's hot cocoa

serves 6

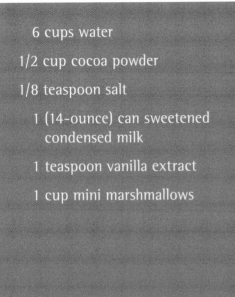

6 cups water

1/2 cup cocoa powder

1/8 teaspoon salt

1 (14-ounce) can sweetened condensed milk

1 teaspoon vanilla extract

1 cup mini marshmallows

1 In a large saucepan, bring water to a boil over high heat. Reduce heat to low and whisk in cocoa powder and salt.

2 Stir in sweetened condensed milk and vanilla; simmer until hot. Remove from heat and serve in mugs topped with mini marshmallows.

Just a Thought:

Take the chill out of a snowy, winter day and welcome them home with a mug of Nana's piping hot cocoa.

notes

index

index